THE LONGMAN BOOK PROJECT

KU-721-492

Fiction
Bands 15–16

Teacher's Resource Book

Literature and Culture

By
Wendy Body
with contributions from Ray Barker, Glenn Franklin and Sue Palmer

LONGMAN

CONTENTS

CONTENTS

Contents

Band 15

Six books for Guided and Independent Reading

Large format Text Extracts for Shared Reading and Shared Writing

Band 16

Six books for Guided and Independent Reading

Large format Text Extracts for Shared Reading and Shared Writing

Copymasters for Bands 15-16

Each title is supported by the following copymasters:

- one Text-level worksheet
- one Word- or Sentence-level worksheet
- author and illustrator information sheets

Review and Response sheets for use with any book

Teacher's Resource Book for Bands 15-16

Contents include:

- advice and suggestions for the Literacy Hour
- book-by-book Teaching Pages
- assessment and monitoring
- additional copymasters for general use

Introduction

First published in 1994, *The Longman Book Project* was conceived as a scheme for use with the whole class and for group teaching. The class- and group-teaching methodology which underpinned *The Longman Book Project* was a far-sighted approach which has proved able to ease the transition to the National Literacy Strategy for the many schools that have adopted the scheme. The fiction strand has now been revised to bring it completely in line with National Literacy Strategy requirements. The major aspects of the KS2 revision to *The Longman Book Project* are:

- the addition of **Text Extracts for Shared Reading and Shared Writing** for whole-class work

- new books added to improve the genre requirements

- new copymasters arranged as Text-, Sentence- and Word-level activities which may be used in class or at home to meet homework requirements

- new **Teacher's Resource Books**: one for each of Years 3–6

- summary grids of suggestions for Text-, Sentence- and Word-level work on the inside back cover of the books.

Bands 15–16 and the National Literacy Strategy

Even such a highly acclaimed scheme as *The Longman Book Project* cannot (and should not) provide you with *everything* you will need to carry out the National Literacy Strategy! However, the nature of the books, accompanying support material and Shared Text Extracts make them an ideal core or framework for use in implementing the National Literacy Strategy teaching approaches and methodology.

Class Teaching

The Text Extracts for Shared Reading and Shared Writing provide a variety of fiction genres and text types. The extracts are laminated for use in text-marking activities and each extract has a shared writing task on the fourth page. The Teaching Pages also offer suggestions for Text-, Sentence- and Word-level work, based on their use.

Guided Reading, Group and Independent Work

The books in Bands 15–16 provide both the lively and appealing content and the variety of language structures and grammar which are necessary in books for Guided Reading at this stage. The Teaching Pages offer suggestions for Text-, Sentence- and Word-level work, and the copymasters for Text, Sentence and Word activities support independent and group work.

You can use Bands 15–16 in two ways:

EITHER: use the books sequentially in the developmental order provided

OR: if you wish the books for Guided Reading to fit in with the Shared Text genre requirements, select titles as in the example below (some titles could be placed in more than one term).

YEAR 6 TERM 1	YEAR 6 TERM 2	YEAR 6 TERM 3
■ Facing the Enemy! Classic Fiction Extracts ■ Weaving Words: poems in different forms	■ Quiddy and the Mysterious Mega Virus ■ Through a Window ■ Escape from Everytown ■ Rich or Poor? ■ Grandfather Singh Stories	■ Myths, Legends and Monsters ■ White Bird Flying ■ On the Day the World Began ■ Tales from the Underland ■ The Quest of Isis

Home-school Links

- Children may, of course, take the books for reading home to parents/carers.

- The copymaster Text, Sentence and Word activities can be used for homework.

- Some of the assessment material may also be shared with parents/carers.

- A copymaster for parents/carers is provided on C9.

Skills Development Summary for Bands 15–16

The books and related materials, including this Teacher's Resource Book, provide extensive teaching and learning support for the following areas required in the National Literacy Strategy objectives:

- comprehension and text response
- appreciation of different genres and types of text
- writing composition
- sentence construction and punctuation skills
- spelling
- vocabulary extension.

The Longman Book Project Fiction Bands 15-16 and the Scottish 5-14 Programme

The 5–14 Reading Attainment Targets at Level E are covered by Fiction Bands 15–16 in conjunction with *The Longman Book Project Non-fiction*.

'At later stages, reading activities should demand that pupils show an overall grasp of a text, an understanding of specific details and how they contribute to the whole, make inferences, supply appropriate supporting evidence, and identify intended audience, purpose and features of style.'

(Guidelines on English Language 5–14, 1991)

Bands 15–16 will make these demands of pupils, presenting them with a variety of challenging, interesting and appropriate texts.

Reading for Enjoyment

The variety of texts in Bands 15–16 will support children in sustaining a personal reading programme by encouraging them to extend the type of texts they read whilst identifying what appeals to them and developing their own reading programme from there. They will be encouraged to share what they have enjoyed and the teacher can take the opportunity to discuss personal reading with individuals.

The variety of texts in Bands 15–16 include science fiction, fantasy, myth and legend, realistic stories, adventure and historical short stories with two poetry books, *Through a Window* and *Weaving Words*, which have poems in a variety of forms, moods and styles.

Reading to Reflect on the Writers' Ideas and Craft

As independent readers, the children reading the texts in Bands 15–16 will be encouraged to make use of previous knowledge and skills to predict content and structure and to locate main points and subsidiary ideas.

The Text-level work and comprehension teaching notes will encourage children to draw analogues between what a text is portraying and their own ideas and feelings. The teacher will lead children to evaluate and make their own judgements. Through the Shared Reading and Writing activities, they will develop the ideas of target audience and writer's purpose.

Awareness of Genre

The breadth and variety of texts in Bands 15–16 give the opportunity for children to explore similarities and differences between stories and poems.

At class and group level they will discuss plot, character, relationships and themes in a variety of genres, covering novels, poems and short stories which will appeal to a divergent group of children.

Reading Aloud

Although there are no targets in this strand at Level E, reading aloud will continue to develop the skills of dramatic expression, reading for effect and performance. Children will be given opportunities to perform by reading, or reciting from memory, a favourite poem or piece of text with a group, class or whole school as the audience.

Knowledge About Language

The comprehensive teaching notes and Text- and Sentence-level work encourage the use of genre as a description of categories of text. *Syllable*, *root*, *stem*, *prefix* and *suffix* can all be explored through the texts in these bands. *Simile* and *metaphor* will be developed through the study of imagery within the texts in Bands 15–16.

Writing

Bands 15–16 have comprehensive teaching notes on Important Principles for Writing that are in line with the Scottish 5–14 Programme for the Development of Writing. Bands 15–16 should meet the demands of Writing Level E.

The Shared Writing tasks can be used to develop the Writing 5–14 Strands *Functional, Personal and Imaginative Writing*, and the variety of texts in Bands 15–16 expose children to models of writing which they can explore and on which they can model their own writing at an appropriate level as they move through the programme.

The teaching notes for each book outline Shared Writing activities that give children ample opportunities to write in each of the above Strands.

The Text-level work in each band gives opportunities for children to examine author style and purpose and a variety of genre. The Guided Writing ideas allow children to develop their own writing in a supported structure.

The Sentence-level work supports Writing 5–14 Strands *Punctuation and Structure* and *Knowledge about Language*. Children are directed to grammar and punctuation in the text being studied and learn the importance of these conventions in writing at all levels. Comprehensive Skills and Strategies checklists match the demands of 5–14 Writing Levels.

Word-level activities direct children to spelling patterns and the composition of words in the text being studied, thus developing skills and strategies for tackling spelling. Skills and Strategies checklists demonstrate that *The Longman Book Project* Fiction Progamme will ensure the demands of the Spelling Strand of 5–14 are well covered at the appropriate levels.

5–14 Strand	5–14 Reading Attainment Targets Level E	The Longman Book Project
Reading for information	Apply the information acquired from a number of different sources for the purpose of a piece of personal research.	Refer to *The Longman Book Project* Non-fiction Strand.
Reading for enjoyment	Read regularly for enjoyment texts with a range of subject matter and provide either orally or in writing a considered personal view of the texts read, supported by some relevant evidence.	A selection of good quality fiction with full-length novels and short stories, both new and traditional, catering for all tastes and a variety of poetry: humorous, traditional and modern.
Reading to reflect on the writer's ideas and craft	Read independently; skim and scan to locate main points of a text; make predictions; identify subsidiary ideas; comment briefly on the opinions and attitudes of the writer; describe, with some direction, the simpler aspects of style and its intended audience.	Teaching notes for each text outline work on comprehension and provide opportunities for experienced readers to examine the text in depth and through the Shared Writing activities.
Awareness of the genre	Identify some similarities and differences of form and content in examples of texts from a variety of genres, and comment on how these reflect the text's purposes.	Fiction Bands 15–16 cover novels, poems, plays and short stories.
Reading aloud	No target for this strand at this level.	Poetry and plays are ideal contexts for encouraging pupils to continue to practise reading aloud in a meaningful way.
Knowledge about language	Show that they know, understand and can use at least the following terms: *genre, syllable, root, stem, prefix, suffix, simile, metaphor*.	Fiction Bands 15–16 contain good examples at this level and the comprehensive teaching notes, Sentence-level and Word-level work give pupils opportunities to extend their knowledge about language.

The Components of Bands 15-16

The upper levels of *The Longman Book Project* Fiction Strand were developed with the following aims in mind:

- to refine and develop children's reading skills, helping them to become critical and responsive readers with a growing level of sophistication and depth of response to books and authors

- to promote children's enthusiasm for books and reading generally, through the study of quality texts written by a large number of established children's authors – offering a rich mix of genres, authorial voices and cultures

- to offer children a wide range of different types of fiction texts through books which have been carefully edited and structured to provide a challenging yet manageable read

- to increase children's awareness of the roles of illustration and presentation in books

- to offer insights into writers and writing, together with books which provide a context for the further development of children's writing skills

- to help children understand how fiction can help self-knowledge, change attitudes and offer insights into life and living

- to begin to consider how a culture can be represented by its literature

- to support teachers in their development of children's reading and writing skills and responses to literature with a teaching approach which is firmly rooted in Best Practice.

The Books

A wide range of distinguished authors and illustrators have contributed to the books in *The Longman Book Project*. These books introduce children to a wide variety of authors' voices and styles and have been critically acclaimed for their quality.

The books can be used:

- for Guided Reading with the teacher

- for group or supported reading with a classroom helper

- as additional books linked by author or theme to the designated Guided Reader for extra reading at home

- for Independent Reading in school.

Each title has a grid on the inside back cover which summarises teaching points that fit the National Literacy Strategy objectives.

As their name implies, the Literature and Culture books have an overall broad theme. They can provide bridges to wider reading and starting points for consideration of how literature represents and reflects particular cultures and aspects of society.

Various literary conventions, genres and themes are represented. For example:

- *Facing the Enemy!* introduces or revisits some of the most famous classic novels through its age-old theme of facing up to adversity or danger.

- The fantasy titles, *Escape from Everytown* and *Quiddy and the Mysterious Mega Virus,* and the poetry books have a variety of social issues at their heart.

- *White Bird Flying*, set in different time periods, has an underlying Christian thread running through its stories.

- The remaining titles are directly rooted in different cultures from various parts of the world and look, in particular, at myths, legends and folk-tales.

Text Extracts for Shared Reading and Shared Writing

Packs 10–12 of the Text Extracts contain extracts from all the books in Bands 15 and 16. Some titles have more than one extract. They have been selected and organised so that each pack contains six extracts which provide examples of the National Literacy Strategy range requirements for the term. They have been designed with optimum text legibility to ensure that the whole class can read the text comfortably.

In 'folded poster' format, the first three pages contain the extract and the fourth provides a related activity or Shared Writing task. Surfaces are laminated so that they can be written on using a *non-permanent* marker or OHP pen.

See Shared Reading and Writing (page 14) for general suggestions as to the use of Text Extracts. Extract-specific suggestions will be found in the Book-by-Book section starting on page 79.

Copymasters for Bands 15–16

For each title, there are:

- two activity sheets for group/independent work, comprising one Sentence- or Word-level sheet and one Text-level sheet. As well as using them in class for group/independent work, the sheets may be used at home to meet homework requirements

- Who's Who? comprises two sheets containing information about the author and/or illustrator who created the book. Sharing this information with children helps to reinforce their understanding of the roles of authors and illustrators. Most of the authors give information about the way they write, and this can also serve as a focus for general discussions about writing and what it involves. In addition, the sheets can be used within a display of a particular author or illustrator's books, or used as a model for children to complete similar profiles about themselves or their classmates as writers and artists.

Also provided are 11 extra Review and Response copymasters which, with one exception, may be used with any book:

Response sheets	*Review sheets – designed for sharing and display*
An Author Study	Myths, Legends and Folktales
An Illustrator Study	A Book for Time Travellers
A Problem to Solve ...	A Cracker to Curl Up With!
What Makes This Character Tick?	Fabulous Fantasy!
Bands 15 and 16: Literature and Culture	A Poem to Please ...
	Stick With This One!

Copymasters in the Teacher's Resource Book

There are 25 additional copymasters in this Teacher's Resource Book.

To support Writing (see pages 41–49)

C1   Ideas I Could Write About Sometime
C2   First Draft Checklist
C3   Borrow an Author's Ideas!
C4   Make a Storyline
C5   Words to Conjure up Characters
C6   Making Things with Words (collecting different kinds of writing)
C7   My Writing Record – cover
C8   My Writing Record – inside (photocopy the two sheets back to back and fold)
C9   Helping Your Child With Writing – Points to Remember

Assessment and Recording (see pages 54–69):

C10   Assessment Sheet 1: Attitudes and Preferences – Reading
C11   Assessment Sheet 2: Attitudes and Preferences – Writing
C12   Assessment Sheet 3: Unaided Writing
C13   Assessment Sheet 4: Understanding of Technical Vocabulary; Synonyms
C14   Assessment Sheet 5: Handwriting
C15   Assessment Sheet 6: Standard English
C16   Oral Reading Behaviour and Strategies
C17   Miscue Analysis
C18   Reading Conference Record
C19   Group Reading Record (Bands 15–16)
C20   Technical Vocabulary: Year 6
C21   Word-level Skills and Strategies: Year 6
C22   Sentence-level Skills and Strategies: Year 6
C23   Text-level Skills and Strategies: Year 6
C24   Progress Certificate: Writer's Award
C25   Progress Certificate: Achievement in Reading

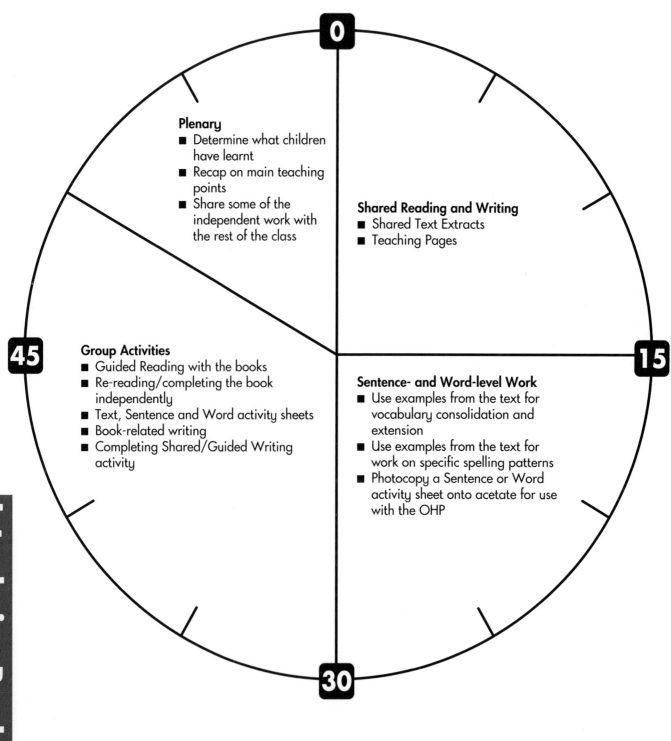

Plenary
- Determine what children have learnt
- Recap on main teaching points
- Share some of the independent work with the rest of the class

Shared Reading and Writing
- Shared Text Extracts
- Teaching Pages

Group Activities
- Guided Reading with the books
- Re-reading/completing the book independently
- Text, Sentence and Word activity sheets
- Book-related writing
- Completing Shared/Guided Writing activity

Sentence- and Word-level Work
- Use examples from the text for vocabulary consolidation and extension
- Use examples from the text for work on specific spelling patterns
- Photocopy a Sentence or Word activity sheet onto acetate for use with the OHP

0

15

30

45

Introducing Bands 15-16

TITLE	AUTHOR
BAND 15	
Grandfather Singh Stories	Pratima Mitchell
Quiddy and the Mysterious Mega Virus	Alison Leonard
Through a Window	Selected by Wendy Body
Rich or Poor?	Pratima Mitchell
Escape from Everytown	Terrance Dicks
Facing the Enemy! Classic Fiction Extracts	Selected by Wendy Body
BAND 16	
Myths, Legends and Monsters	Mick Gowar
White Bird Flying	Nicholas Orme
On the Day the World Began	Geraldine McCaughrean
Tales from the Underland	Dennis Hamley
The Quest of Isis	Geraldine McCaughrean
Weaving Words: poems in different forms	Selected by David Orme

Shared Reading and Shared Writing with the Whole Class

Using the Text Extracts for Shared Reading and Shared Writing

As children progress with their reading, the Text Extracts will enable you to consolidate and extend the following skills:

- comprehension and text response to a range of genres
- spelling patterns
- punctuation
- the structure and organisation of sentences
- writing
- checking reading strategies.

Suggestions for using specific extracts will be found on the appropriate Teaching Pages (see pages 79–110). The following suggestions are for *general* use.

For Shared Reading and Writing sessions, it is advisable to have the following readily available:

- *non-permanent* pens to mark or highlight individual words, part-words, phrases, etc.
- Blu-Tack or Post-It notes to mask words, e.g. when revising the use of context to deal with unfamiliar words or creating an 'instant' cloze text
- paper for Shared Writing and blank word cards.

Shared Reading

- Read the extract with the class. Read with good pace and expression and point to the words using a pointer while reading.
- Identify the genre.
- Explore and extend children's understanding through discussion and differentiated questioning.
- Talk about the characters, setting and events, recalling and referring back to the text and encouraging children to draw on their own experiences.
- Re-read sentences/sections to confirm responses to questions and points made in discussion.
- Discuss any textual features such as the rhyming schemes in poems or the layout of plays.
- Predict what might happen next or what might have gone before.
- The extracts are laminated and are therefore suitable for text-marking activities using a *non-permanent* pen.

Examples of Text-marking Activities

- Underline, for example: key words/phrases, language features and stylistic devices such as metaphors, 'The part which tells us about ...'

- Ring or mark, for example: particular spelling patterns, punctuation marks, designated parts of speech, compound words, syllables in words.

- Annotate the text, for example: inserting adverbs, adjectives or stage directions, labelling the main idea in a paragraph.

The Activity Section

Each extract has a related activity, linked to the National Literacy Strategy teaching objectives, to complete with the class as part of your Shared Text work. These are essentially Shared Writing tasks, e.g. a character portrait, writing dialogue or writing in the style of the author, but there are also some which have a Sentence- or Word-level activity, e.g. punctuating a passage in different ways or writing definitions of words used in the extract.

Shared Writing Tasks

- You may not always wish to complete the writing with the whole class; it can be started off with the class and then finished by groups or individuals in Guided or Independent Writing.

- It is advisable to have some large sheets of paper to hand to continue the writing if there is insufficient space on the poster.

- It is suggested that you use the activity section for drafting and revising any Shared Writing, and that a final version is produced on paper so that it may be kept for children to re-read. This final version could, of course, be written out or keyed in by children instead of the teacher.

Examples of Additional Text-related Activities

Text-level Examples

- Ask children to locate particular parts of the text, e.g. *The part which tells us about ...*

- Discuss characters and settings.

- Revise, check or teach technical vocabulary.

- Identify and discuss the rhyming scheme and/or structure of a poem.

- Select response activities from the examples starting on page 26.

- Use the text as a stimulus for additional Shared Writing and as a model for pupils' own writing.

Sentence-level Examples

- Discuss any special features, e.g. imperatives for stage directions.

- Identify and discuss the punctuation and how it affects the way we read.

- Identify and discuss connectives and joining phrases.

- Focus on verb tenses and agreement.

- Change direct speech into reported speech.

- Identify and discuss where commas mark embedded clauses.

Word-level Examples

- Identify letter strings in particular words and generate other examples. By writing the new words on separate cards, you can use them later for group revision or hold the cards up to do a Look-Say-Remove-Spell-Check activity with the class.

- Highlight particular words and find synonyms.

- Find examples of words with particular spelling patterns.

- Highlight and discuss unfamiliar or unusual words.

- Look for words within words, e.g. *ate* in *fortunate*.

- Find examples of compound words and contracted word forms, e.g. *we're*.

- Identify and mark syllables and designated prefixes or suffixes.

Obviously, the Text Extracts for Shared Reading and Shared Writing cannot provide you with all the Shared Texts you need! Pelican Big Books (published by Longman) offer a range of big books which can be used at Year 6 – see the examples below.

Pelican Big Books for Bands 15–16

TITLE	GENRE	YEAR 6
■ Character Portraits	Anthology: extracts for character study	Term 1
■ A Collection of Classic Poems	Poetry: famous classic poems	
■ Discoveries ... Extracts from Classic Novels	Anthology: classic fiction linked by theme	
■ An Introduction to A Midsummer Night's Dream	Shakespeare: play extracts, background	
■ Writers' Lives	Non-fiction: biography and autobiography	
■ Discoveries ... Extracts from Classic Novels	Anthology: classic fiction linked by theme	Term 2
■ Poets writing in a variety of forms	Poetry in different forms	
■ Prayers and Poems From Around the World	Multi cultural anthology	
■ Descriptive Settings	Longer established descriptive writing	
■ Issues in the News	News reports, discussion text	
■ A World War II Anthology	Anthology, prose and poetry	Term 3
■ Festivals	Non-fiction: RE	
■ The Human Body	Non-fiction: science	
■ Greek and Roman Gods and Heroes: an encyclopedia	Reference: specialised encyclopedia	
■ Poems to Compare and Contrast	Poetry linked by theme or poet	
■ Words Borrowed from Other languages	Non-fiction: reference, word origins	

Shared Reading and Shared Writing

Shared Writing

To become effective writers, children need to read and experience a wide range of books, with teachers helping them to recognise the different ways in which authors organise writing and structure it according to their purpose.

Children have to learn that writing is a means of communication, with a message and a purpose, and that it is the purpose and the audience which determine the form and style. They also have to learn the conventions of spelling, punctuation, grammar and layout.

Children need to have an understanding of the processes of writing and plenty of opportunities to experiment and explore with a range of genres – and they best learn about genre and process through teacher modelling, commentary and discussion. It is only when children understand the purposes and structures of various genres that they can make appropriate choices for their own writing.

In short, children learn best to write through exposure to the models of writing provided by sharing books and participating in Shared and Guided Writing, and then by writing and experimenting for themselves.

Shared Writing teaches children:

- to consider audience, purpose and form
- how to generate and record ideas
- how to structure a piece of writing
- how to revise, review, edit and publish

while developing and consolidating spelling and presentation skills.

Some Advantages of Shared Writing

Shared Writing builds children's confidence and motivation because:

- the burdens of simultaneous transcription and composition are eased for developing writers
- it is a joint effort so there is no question of failure or frustration
- everyone's opinion and contribution – no matter how small – is valued
- there are no right or wrong answers – changing your mind is part of the process
- strategies for dealing with problems are taught and modelled
- collaboration is presented as a desirable and acceptable means of working.

The skills of writing are taught in context.

- The importance of audience and purpose are made explicit.
- Discussion and modelling develop awareness of style and grammar.
- Phonic and spelling knowledge is consolidated and developed: *How should I spell that? Does that look right?*
- The emphasis is on sense and meaning, which encourages children to be critical and alert to problems.
- Creative and imaginative use of language is encouraged and demonstrated.

In addition to acting as the scribe, the teacher's role is to model, explain, comment on and discuss aspects of the writing. It is important to share your thought processes and help to take the writing on by posing appropriate questions.

Apart from showing what to do when problems arise, the teacher can model and draw children's attention to the technicalities of spelling, grammar, punctuation and layout conventions and, of course, demonstrate the process stages of: prepare, write, revise, edit, publish and evaluate.

Planning for Shared Writing

Before Writing

- Discuss the audience and purpose.

- Discuss what form the writing will take – story, report, etc.

- Brainstorm ideas, possible openings, points to include, etc.

During Writing

- Remember that it is the children's composition and not yours – although you will help to shape and direct the writing. It is all too easy to take over from the children in the heat of the creative moment!

- Demonstrate and discuss:
  - writing conventions, e.g. layout, punctuation, grammatical features such as tense agreement
  - appropriate and varied language use, e.g. sentence structure, word choices, examples of figurative language
  - spelling strategies
  - features of the particular text type, e.g. the language of instructions, key points presented as bullets, story structure, first or third person narrative, use of structural marker words/phrases, e.g. *First we, Finally*.
  - handwriting and use of features such as underlining or words in capitals or colour
  - how posing questions can help to take the writing on.

- Make process aspects explicit by demonstrating:
  - re-reading as writing continues, attending to meaning, checking for sense and the effect being created
  - ongoing revision, e.g. going back to a previous sentence to add or make changes in the light of what has just been written
  - highlighting or making notes for later changes.
  - ensure the writing is not hijacked by a vociferous minority! All the children should feel able to make contributions.

After Writing

- Revise and edit to check clarity of meaning, add details, descriptions, etc. and to see that audience and purpose demands have been met.

- Proofread for spelling, punctuation and grammatical errors and omissions.

- Discuss what children have learned from the writing and recap on important teaching points.

- Publish, for example as a wall story, read to another class, make into a book, clip to other sheets of Shared Writing to hang in the classroom for children to revisit.

The Text Extracts can be used in a variety of ways to lead into Shared Writing. For example:

- Create your own verses for rhymes and poems.

- Use information from the text to build a character portrait.

- Write a suitable back cover blurb for the story.

- Discuss and list ideas for a sequel to a story.

- Rewrite the first section of a story as a character's diary.

- Compose letters to the author or illustrator.

- Discuss the setting, then write a description.

- Write reasons for and against a particular course of action.

- Write in the role of characters in the book, for example:
  - diary extracts
  - continuation of the story
  - letters to and from characters.

The Teaching Pages for individual titles (pages 79–109) all have suggestions for Shared Writing activities.

The Writing Process – a Summary

You can help children to learn about the craft and processes of writing by ensuring that they become familiar with the stages that are involved in producing any important piece of writing:

1 Starting Writing/Planning

- This is the preliminary stage of getting ideas of what to write about.

- Children can be helped in several ways:
  - discussions as a class, with a group or with friends
  - referring to the list of titles/topics being recorded on **C1**
  - brainstorming
  - visualising a character or a setting
  - flow diagrams
  - spider diagrams or topic webs
  - going on an 'Observer's Walk' around the local area
  - encouraging pairs of children to brainstorm five story ideas or titles which are then written on separate cards. All the ideas may be kept together in a box for future reference/browsing, perhaps under category or genre headings.

- There may be something written on a piece of paper to guide the writing as a result of this stage, but it is not necessary.

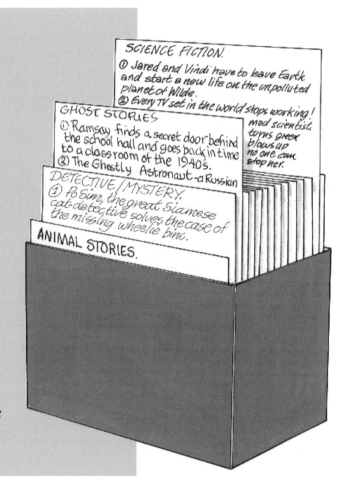

2 Drafting

- The writing of continuous text. The point here is to get something down on paper which is legible. Spelling and other presentation skills are not crucial at this stage.

- Children should be encouraged to 'have a go' at spelling unknown words and not stop to look them up or ask for the correct spellings.

- Spelling lines can be useful: children write as much of the word as they can and put a line for the part they don't know.

3 Revising

- During this stage, the child reads the text and ask questions like:
  - *Does it make sense?*
  - *Have I said what I meant to say?*
  - *Have I missed anything out?*
  - *Does it sound right?*

- Help children to understand the purpose of this stage by pointing out:
  - to **revise** is to **review** and **review** means to **see again**
  - **revise** is like the word **revisit** – we **revisit** what we have written.

- During this stage, the writing is likely to be shared with someone else, if the writer wishes:
  - friends
  - a group at a similar stage in their writing
  - the teacher.

- Writing is shared in order to get someone else's opinion and advice on how the content might be improved.

- This stage is likely to result in a text which has comments, crossings-out, asterisks and additions, insertions, chunks physically cut out and fixed elsewhere, etc. It is important that children understand that revising does not have to mean rewriting.

- It is always advisable to leave some time (e.g. at least a day) between the writing of the first draft and its revision.

4 Editing/Proofreading

- This is the stage at which careful attention is paid to the spelling and punctuation.

- This is best done:
  - in pairs or small groups
  - with the aid of word sources and dictionaries, and the teacher, if additional support is required.

5 Publishing

- The final version of the text is prepared: typed, printed or handwritten according to the purpose of the writing and how it is to be made public.

- Publishing simply means to make public in some way. The outcome could be, for example:
  - a letter to send off
  - a sheet for a wall display
  - a book (in which case decisions as to pagination [page order], layout and illustrations, etc. have to be made).

6 Evaluation

- The writer is helped to evaluate what he or she has done:
  - What is the child's opinion of the completed work?
  - What has he or she learned from it?
  - Is there anything he or she would tackle differently when doing a similar piece of writing?

7 Points to Remember

- Not every piece of writing a child does will go through all these stages, simply because they are not always appropriate and they are clearly time-consuming.

- Some pieces of writing are not worth the effort of reworking, particularly if they were originally done on an 'off day' or children are not really interested in them. Children should be encouraged to *choose* for themselves the writing they will develop in some way.

- Some children will be reluctant to carry out this process; encourage them to choose one piece of writing from among the most recent five or six pieces they have done for further refinement.

- Sharing your writing with someone else can be a painful process and one that is counter-productive if it is not handled sensitively. You can model the kinds of thoughtful and positive questions and comments which are needed when you:
  - respond to children's written work
  - are doing Shared Writing with a group or the class.

- You can also establish ground rules and guidelines for sharing (displayed on a chart on the wall). The main rule should always be:

  *Tell the writer something you really like about the writing and **then** see if you can suggest anything that will make it even better.*

Guided Reading and Independent Work

Using the Books for Guided Reading

You will need one copy of the book for each member of the group. It is a good idea to have an extra copy for yourself which is clearly labelled 'Teacher's Copy'. You can then annotate and highlight this copy as a permanent reminder of the points and work you need to cover – as well as adding to the grid on the inside back cover.

Where children are partway through a text, recap on what has already been read before guiding them through the next or remaining section. Alternatively, introduce the book and guide children through the section to be read, e.g. by looking at the illustrations, encouraging predictions, discussing unfamiliar vocabulary and concepts, and establishing a feel for the storyline. Whenever possible, give children a focus for the section to be read, e.g. *How does Character X change in this chapter?*

Children then read the text independently, at their own speed, silently or aloud, with you monitoring, supporting or prompting where necessary. You may wish to provide a task for faster readers, e.g. *Write down any words you found difficult. Note down how Character X changes.*

Discuss the book and any features related to your lesson focus (e.g. how authors build and describe settings) before, if appropriate, re-reading part of the text in unison for expression and pace. The Guided Reading session can then be followed up on that or subsequent days with the related copymasters – both in school and at home.

Working with a group of children as opposed to individuals has several advantages. For example:

- Through discussion of each other's responses and interpretations, children reach a better understanding of the text and clarify individual misinterpretations.

- Plot, characters, genre, use of language, etc. can be explored more fully through a shared, rather than individual, response.

- Children have greater opportunities to refer to a text to support their opinions and conclusions and therefore develop their ability to do so.

- The support of the group helps individuals to gain confidence in interpreting and dealing with texts.

- The ongoing exposure to other children's responses and reflections gives individual pupils insights into tackling texts which they can then apply in private reading.

- The group re-reading provides opportunities to practise reading with varied pace, expression and fluency, and weaker readers in the group will have support and good models of reading with expression.

Independent Group Work

The most difficult part of managing the Literacy Hour is the time when the teacher is working on Guided Reading or Guided Writing with one group while the rest of the class work independently.

The class can be organised in different ways, perhaps on different days. For example, children can work individually but on the same task, e.g. writing a story; they can work individually within a group, e.g. writing a character portrait or completing an activity sheet linked to their group reading; or they can work in pairs, e.g. on a text-marking activity. Many teachers find that a carousel model, in which activities are rotated around the groups, is still the easiest to manage – providing that the activities allow for differentiation.

Working with a class of 30 in five groups matched for ability could produce the following structure for a week. This would obviously change where teachers are working with only one group a day.

	MONDAY	TUESDAY	WEDNESDAY	THURSDAY	FRIDAY
Group 1	**Guided Reading**	Book-related activity sheets	**Guided Writing**	Word or sentence work	Independent Writing
Group 2	**Guided Writing**	Word or sentence work	Independent Writing	**Guided Reading**	Book-related activity sheets
Group 3	Independent Writing	**Guided Reading**	Book-related activity sheets	**Guided Writing**	Word or sentence work
Group 4	Book-related activity sheets	**Guided Writing**	Word or sentence work	Independent Writing	**Guided Reading**
Group 5	Word or sentence work	Independent Writing	**Guided Reading**	Book-related activity sheets	**Guided Writing**

There are some obvious implications for managing group and independent work, as follows.

- If possible, try to arrange for additional adult helpers, e.g. parents to oversee lower ability groups working on more challenging activities.

- If children still need it, have a physical reminder that you are not to be disturbed unless absolutely necessary, e.g. a *Do-Not-Disturb* speech bubble cartoon or notice.

- Some classes may still need similar physical reminders for each group's table, e.g. *Independent and Quiet Work in Progress!*

- Ensure that all the groups know what they are doing and what they should do if they finish early by using a task board with instructions.

Responding to Fiction Texts

Having achieved a good level of reading competence, Year 6 is the time not only to consolidate and extend children's literacy skills but also to sustain and extend the love of books which, it is hoped, has been developed during earlier years.

The overall Text-level teaching aims should be:

- to promote and foster children's enthusiasm for reading

- to ensure that children read with understanding, and are able to deduce and infer meanings

- to develop children's interactions with texts – especially their personal responses to writing, ideas and illustrations

- to encourage children's awareness of what writers and illustrators are trying to achieve and how individual texts are structured

- to develop children's ability to support their opinions and interpretations by reference to appropriate sections of the text

- to help children appreciate significant aspects of a text and to determine which aspects are more important than others

- to enable children to experience a wide range of different genres and help them to become aware of the characteristics of different types of fiction texts.

The following pages contain activities and suggestions, both to promote enjoyment of books and to develop children's responses to fiction. They are followed by copymasters which can be used with *any* book.

Suggested Activities for Group and Independent Work

Activities for Adult-led Groups

- Discuss if and how the story/poem has changed children's thinking or point of view in any way.

- Encourage children to describe their feelings at various points in the story. Do they change? How, when and why?

- Discuss the message or moral of the story.

- Discuss characters – their appearance, personality, relationships, actions and behaviour.

- Identify and discuss what happens to a character in the course of a story. Does s/he change in any way? How?

- Consider what characters might be thinking/saying at various points:
  - Use Post-It notes to add thought/speech bubbles to illustrations.
  - Use a sheet of acetate clipped to the page and a *non-permanent* pen to add thought/speech bubbles.
  - Discuss and contrast what is said with what might be thought.

- Sitting in the 'Hot Seat' – a child or adult takes on the role of a character to answer questions posed by other children.

- Identify cause and effect by constructing a two-column table. For example:

This is what happened	This is what made it happen

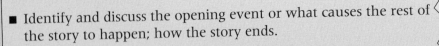

- Identify and discuss the opening event or what causes the rest of the story to happen; how the story ends.

- Identify/underline, using acetate, 'the part which says/tells you about ...'

- Identify and discuss the physical and temporal settings of the story. Which features of the physical setting are essential to the story? Which might simply have been added by the illustrator?

- Identify and discuss the cultural setting. What gives the reader the sense of a particular culture in both text and illustration? How might the story change if it took place in a different cultural setting?

- Compare and contrast settings and the ways they are depicted in different books, e.g. those set by the sea, those with fantasy settings.

- Questions for discussion about the illustration:
  - What has the illustrator added to the text in terms of extra details?
  - What do children like/dislike about the way the illustrator has portrayed the main characters?
  - Can children spot any distinctive features in the illustrator's style: the way people are drawn, for example?

- Cloze exercises, where the deletions focus on aspects of the author's use of language, e.g. rhyme, onomatopoeia.

- Using acetate over the text, underline and discuss memorable or unusual words and phrases.

- Discuss alternative wordings an author could have used.

Independent Activities

- Write in the role of characters in the book, e.g. letters to and from characters.

- Make a family tree for characters, perhaps extending it to include other generations who do not feature in the story.

- Write a list of requirements (e.g. costume, make-up, props, wig) for the actor who might play the part of a character in a film.

- Make a storyboard for part of a film of the book.

- Cloze, where the text deletions are, for example, adjectives or rhymes.

- Using acetate over the text, underline memorable or unusual words and phrases for later comparison and discussion.

- Prediction – put a paperclip or rubber band around the pages following the point at which you want the child to stop reading and tell you what he or she thinks might happen next.

- Understanding of story structure:
  - sequence main events or chunks of text
  - design flow charts of main events/actions
  - draw pictures to show the sequence of the story/make a storyboard.

- Write three things that one character might think about another.

- Describe what a child character might be like when s/he grows up.

- Write stories using characters from more than one book.

- Complete a book review sheet.

- Write a description of the setting.

- Change dialogue into playscript.

- Write an alternative ending to the story.

- Extend the story, e.g. *This book finishes on page 48. What do you think the author could have written if s/he had had one more page to fill at the end?*

- Keep a reading log in which responses and opinions can be jotted down after reading a book in class or at home. Like a writing journal, this is not marked but simply discussed with the teacher and/or other children.

Question Cards

Text-response questions, such as those below, can be written on individual cards: as reminders for you, to initiate a class discussion, for groups to prepare an oral presentation or discussion which can be recorded and played back for the rest of the class, or to use as a stimulus for writing.

- Is there a moment in the book when you would like to help one of the characters? What could you do?

- Do you admire a particular character in the book so much that you wish you were like him or her?

- Do you think you have anything in common with any of these characters? What?

- How close is the main character's personality to someone you know in real life?

- What would you have done if, like the main character(s), you had been faced with this or a similar situation?

- Is there anything special that you have learned from reading this book?

- Has this book taught you anything about being part of a different culture from your own?

- Have you learned anything about the way people should try to behave from reading this book?

- Is there anything a particular character says or does which makes you agree or disagree strongly with what is said or done?

- Would you like to live in the time or place in which this book is set?

- Did this book make you feel as if you were part of the story when you were reading it, or did you feel as if you were on the outside looking in? Why?

- What is your opinion of the way this book is written?

- Choose a poem from the collection. What is it that gives the poem its impact and makes it so effective?

- What do you think it would be like if one of the characters in the book came to stay with you for a few days? Would it be a good visit or a disturbing one? Why?

- Does this book raise any issues with which we should all be concerned?

- Have you learned anything about other places from this book?
- Did you find yourself taking sides with any of the characters in the book? Which one(s) and why?
- Has this book influenced the way you think about anything?
- What do you think the author was trying to achieve in this book?
- Given the opportunity, what would you change about this book?
- What evidence can you find in the book that proves a character acted foolishly or wrongly?
- What is it about the design of the book which makes you want to read it?
- What category, genre or type of fiction does this book fit? What other books of this type do you know?
- Choose a poem from this collection. What message is the poet trying to give us?
- Did your feelings change as you were reading this book? In what way and at what points?
- If you were able to ask the author why he or she had written this book, what do you think the reply would be?
- Was there anything which you found challenging when you read this book?
- Would you want to buy this book for yourself? Why/Why not?
- Did this book raise any questions in your mind as you were reading it?
- Which section or chapter of the book did you find the most satisfying? Why?
- What kind of voices do you think the main characters might have? Why?
- What questions would you want to ask someone else who has read this book?
- How do you think one of the characters in the book would explain his or her behaviour to (a) an enemy and (b) a friend?
- Does this book remind you of any others you have read? How?

Guided and Independent Writing

Guided Writing offers the opportunity for the teacher to work closely and regularly with a group of children in order to improve and extend their writing skills. Children are grouped according to their ability and the writing is usually linked to the group's reading or to the Shared Reading and Writing which has been done with the class.

The teacher selects the writing focus, e.g. a letter or story opening, and discusses purpose and audience. Children in the group write individually, with the teacher giving support, feedback and clarification with regard to: spelling, writing conventions (e.g. punctuation and layout), features of the particular text type, vocabulary, handwriting, process aspects (e.g. re-reading to maintain flow and meaning, revising and making changes, and editing). In other words, a session may involve:

- planning a piece of writing
- supporting writing that is already in progress
- evaluating and improving a piece.

The writing may be shared with the rest of the class during the plenary session.

Writers' Workshop

As children become more proficient writers, however, there will not be sufficient time for extended writing within the standard organisational pattern of the Literacy Hour. One way of solving this problem is to set up a **Writers' Workshop**, an established approach which has been used with equal success alongside the Literacy Hour. One of the underlying concepts is to give writing special status; another is that by treating children *as* authors they are more likely to *behave* as authors.

Writers' Workshop has a very similar structure to the Literacy Hour and should take place once every week or two weeks. There should be an emphasis on child-selected writing because the children must feel they have ownership of their writing. You may decide to determine the form (story, recount, poem, etc.), but the children should select the content. Alternatively, you may select the topic to fit in with range requirements, e.g. Imagined Worlds, but the children should choose the form. In the description below, the timings are approximate and will vary with year groups.

A Format for a Writers' Workshop

Part 1: The Class Mini-lesson/Introduction (5 minutes)

Focus on one of three main categories linking into what you have been doing in the Literacy Hour:

- *Purpose and form*, e.g. stories for a particular audience, reminders of genre options.
- *Mechanics*, e.g. punctuation, topic-specific vocabulary.
- *Content*, e.g. brainstorming ideas, possible plots.

Part 2: Individual Writing Time (30—45 minutes)

Establish ground rules to make this time as productive as possible. For example:

- Start by reading through what you wrote last time. Continue with that piece if you have more to say. If not, start a new one.

- No talking at all for the first five or ten minutes. After that you may talk softly but *only* about writing.

- Don't stop to ask/look for spellings. Have a go or use a spelling line. If you hit a real problem, put up your hand and wait for the teacher to come.

Part 3: Preparing for Publication (10—15 minutes)

During this time children may, for example, be:
- discussing a first draft with a friend/group
- revising the current piece
- editing the current piece
- keying in the final text
- working out pagination, etc. if the final outcome is to be a book
- illustrating their own or someone else's writing
- continuing with writing if that is the most important thing at this time.

NB: With experienced children, some teachers prefer to run Parts 2 and 3 as one.

Part 4: The Sharing Time (10 minutes)

- Ask which children at draft or revision stage would like to share their work with the class.

- The children take turns to sit in the Author's Chair and read their work. The Author's Chair can be a specially painted and decorated old wooden chair, or your chair which has a fabric drape thrown over it (e.g. an old sheet which children have painted with words, letters, books, authors' names, etc. using fabric paints).

- The rest of the class comment and question – within the framework of the How to Help an Author guidelines below. The guidelines should be displayed in the room.

- Make time at some stage to have a few words with children who have shared their work to see if and how it has helped them.

- Use the Author's Chair at special Writers' Storytimes to share published work – the child reads to the class or sits in the chair while you read his or her writing to the class.

How to Help an Author ...
- Listen carefully to what the author is reading or saying.
- Say what it is that you really like about the writing.
- Ask questions if there was anything you didn't understand.
- Say if there was something you would like to know which the author didn't mention.
- Say *I was a bit confused when you said ...* if there was something which didn't make sense to you.
- Tell the author where you thought the choice of words was really good.
- Let the author know if there is something you think he or she could do to make the writing even better. (Note use of the word 'even'!)

Helping Children to Consider Characters and Settings

'Good stories are like good sandwiches …

The bread is no good without the filling, but the filling is no good without the bread!'

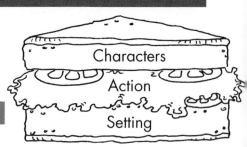

Characters

There are four main aspects to think about when creating characters:

- physical appearance

- approximate age

- personality

- hero or villain.

Children need to practise creating characters and writing descriptions – initially working with you in Guided Writing. Help them to create stronger, more 'alive' characters by considering and discussing the following basic questions:

- All humans have the same basic features, yet every one is different. What is it that makes *this* character unique?

- Do I want to tell the reader everything all at once or give details as the story develops? For example:
  – *She turned the page with a grimy, wrinkled finger.*
  – *He ran as fast as he could on chubby little legs.*

- What would I do/say/think/feel if I was in this situation? How would I move/react/speak?

- Can I *show* the reader what my character is feeling, rather than simply saying it? For example:
  – *She could feel her heart begin beating faster and faster.*
  – *He tried to shout with a voice that had suddenly disappeared.*

- Can I use metaphors or similes to make descriptions more vivid? For example:
  – *His voice rumbled like an angry thunderstorm.*

- Is it better to add details and description after the first draft? For example:
  – *What have I told the reader?*
  – *What could I tell the reader?*

Character Checklist

Characters will only appear 'real' to the reader if they are 'real' to the writer. Whether or not all the aspects below feature in the actual writing, children should nevertheless consider them when they are creating a character. The more important the character is in a story, the more important it is to flesh out the detail.

Main/supporting character
Age
Gender
Colour/colouring
Facial features
Hair
Build and height
Clothes
General appearance (e.g. small and scruffy)
How he/she/it speaks
How he/she/it moves
Family/background
Personality
Likes/dislikes (e.g. hobbies)
Hero/villain – all good or all bad?

Settings

Any real consideration of setting is often neglected by young writers. Considering the following basic questions will help them to improve their story-writing skills.

- Is the story set in the past, present or future?

- Is it a real or fantasy setting?

- What is the main physical setting? A city? A forest?

- How essential is the setting to the storyline? The more essential it is, the clearer the picture created for the reader needs to be.

- Will the setting change during the story? How?

- What are the obvious features of the place?

- Is it daytime or night-time? How does this affect the way the setting looks?

- How might the setting affect the way characters move/behave?

- Are there particular sounds/smells/sights associated with the setting? Will they change in different weather conditions?

- Is the setting familiar or strange to the characters and readers? The more unfamiliar it is, the clearer the picture created for the reader needs to be.

- Is it better to add details and description after the first draft? For example:
  – What *have* I told the reader?
  – What *could* I tell the reader?

- What descriptive details can be included to make the setting 'come alive'?

Creating a Character's and Setting Reference

Here are some examples of useful tasks for Guided and Independent Writing related to characters and settings. These could be kept in a separate notebook for later reference.

- Brainstorm and list phrases, similes and metaphors to describe: hair, eyes, expression height, weight, skin colour etc.

- Build up a Character Gallery of stock characters (one per page) of: an old man, an old woman, a young girl, a young boy, a baby, a mum, a dad, a grandmother, a grandfather, a girl your age, a boy your age, a pet dog/cat, a giant, a bully, a king, a queen, etc.

- Brainstorm and list phrases, similes and metaphors to describe: anger, fear, happiness, relief, sadness, anxiety.

- Create a character – over a period of time – who can be used in several stories.

- Identify and list common settings (e.g. a city, a forest, the countryside, a castle, space, the sea, a school, etc.) together with their expected features and attributes – sounds, sights and smells.

- Brainstorm and list phrases, similes and metaphors to describe: night, day, dusk, early morning, different weather conditions.

- Past/present/future settings: list main indicators, e.g. clothes, transport, buildings.

Crunch Questions!

- Have I created a real and believable character?

- Will my readers care about what happens to my character?

- At the end of the story, might readers feel that they have met and got to know a new person/creature?

- If my readers asked me questions about my character, would I be able to answer them?

- Have I created a real and believable setting?

- Will my readers be able to imagine what the place looks like?

Responding to Children's Writing

In Year 6, teachers should be expecting children to take responsibility for what they are writing and to demonstrate reasonable critical awareness of their own work. You can build on this through the way you respond to what children are trying to do, aiming, by your questioning, to make them think about their writing and to give them insights into what they should be considering. Examples of some questions which teachers have found useful are shown below.

Starter Questions

- *What's your writing about?*
- *What started you off on this?*
- *Which is your favourite part?*
- *Which part is most important to you?*
- *Shall I tell you what I really liked about your writing?*

Follow-on Questions

These are usually re-statements, such as *You said you ...*, and are designed to encourage the child to give more information. For example:

- I'd really like to know more about ... how they found the way home. Did they have to ...?

- Do you think you've told your readers everything they will want to know about: character's name/setting/what happened, etc.

Process-related Questions

- What do you want to do next?
- Are you going to develop this (part)? How might you do it?
- How do you feel about the beginning/end/etc.?
- How does your title fit your story?
- Can you think of a different way of saying this?
- Is there anything I can help you with?
- Did you find any part where it was difficult to say what you wanted to?
- What do you want your readers to think/feel when they read this part?
- Are there any parts where you are really pleased with your choice of words?
- Are there any parts where you're not really satisfied?
- Do you want to share this with the class? Would it help you in any way to do so?

Some Golden Rules

- Treat children as writers and they are more likely to behave as writers.
- Make time to celebrate children's achievements.
- Give children plenty of time for writing – all writers need practice.
- Help children to find real and varied audiences.
- Provide a rich and varied reading diet.
- Encourage writing for genuine, personally significant purposes.
- Help children to understand process, use a staged approach to working at selected pieces of writing.
- Encourage reflection and self-evaluation.
- Respond to content, not simply the technical skills of writing.
- Encourage discussion, collaboration and peer group support.
- Create the best writing environment possible.
- Involve parents in what you are trying to do.
- Try to make writing a really high status activity.

A classroom to encourage writers has ...

- large sheets of paper for Shared Writing
- a variety of writing implements
- different colours, shapes and sizes of paper
- a range of dictionaries, word sources and a thesaurus (both published and class-produced)
- a message board and class postbox
- word boards, e.g. **Words of the Week; Amazing Adjectives!**
- a class diary to record interesting happenings
- frequently changed displays of writing
- a 'Poetree' – display children's poems on leaf shapes tied to branches
- an 'Authors of the Week' board with self-portraits, biographical details and examples of writing from three or four children at a time
- reminder lists/display of the different genres of writing, e.g. stories, poems, jokes, reports, plays, instructions, recipes, messages, diaries, etc
- guidelines on 'How to help a writer', i.e. responding to each other's work
- an appropriately decorated old chair – the Author's Chair – where children sit to read their work to the class.

Writers on Writing ...

Many of *The Longman Book Project* authors have made comments
about their work. Below are a selection of these which could be
used to initiate a class discussion on writing.

Stories are everywhere, all the
time, but you have to train
yourself to look for them. I often
start with some very trivial thing
and ask myself Who/What/
When/Where/Why and then
What next? questions about it.

Martin Waddell

When I'm stuck, I set a timer and
give myself 20 minutes to write
one page. It doesn't matter what I
write, just as long as I write.

Mark Ezra

Write what you know about – that's what they
told me at school. It was the silliest advice I was
ever given and I never followed it. If I'd waited
to know enough about anything, I wouldn't
ever have started.

Geraldine McCaughrean

Everyone likes to make
something: a cake, a model, a
painting, a chair ... I like to make
something with words.

Judith Nicholls

The first thing that happens when I start writing
a story is that a picture comes into my head ...

Adèle Geras

My first and second drafts are done in
pen (fearful crossings out and messiness),
third, fourth, fifth (usually – sometimes
more) on the word processor.

Dennis Hamley

It rolled in front of me like a red uncut
carpet. All I had to do was cut and snip
so it was right for kids to walk down it
and see what they want to.

Lemn Sissay

I fill scraps of paper, notebooks,
etc. with ideas for the future. I
never move without a piece of
paper attached to me somewhere.
If I had to sit down at a blank
sheet and wonder what to do, I
would never write.

Agnes Szudek

I write as a way of exploring things:
exploring what I've experienced, what
I feel and think about things and the
words I use. It is a way of looking at
the world afresh and discovering and
being surprised by connections and
patterns.

John Cotton

I work on an Apple Mac computer and rewrite
and rewrite and rewrite.

Laurence Staig

When I started writing it was only about my life, now I want to write about other people's lives, so I research by talking to people everywhere. Poets are all individuals, the only thing we SHOULD have in common is HONESTY.

Benjamin Zephaniah

I can write anywhere – in the street, on the bus, out with my dog. I carry a notebook with me wherever I go.

Primrose Lockwood

The great thing is, never limit yourself. Anything might get a poem going, if you are alert … Keep awake, and there are poems everywhere.

Fred Sedgwick

I like to work at my desk with familiar things around me. Every now and then I get up to walk around the room, fidget with various objects, then sit down again. It's all part of the way I concentrate.

John Mole

As a child I always made up stories in my head at night in bed as I was going to sleep. My bed was a safe place to go adventuring, and so was the inside of my head.

Alison Leonard

I like to play with an idea in my head for quite some time before I begin to write. I think the idea through and try to picture settings and characters. After an initial general plan, I plot each chapter. I may change things as I go along but I think the planning stage for story writing is very important. I always write a brief character study for the main characters so that I really get to know them.

David Webb

If I'm stuck for an idea, I climb into a hot bubble bath, close my eyes and visualise pictures inside my head. The pictures join up together and form a story with a beginning, middle and end. I jump out, eat a packet of chocolate digestives, and write down the words to fit the pictures to form the story.

Sally-Ann Lever

What's exciting is having the idea in the first place and that lovely, crazy, scribbly stage when the ideas are tumbling onto the page – that's the best bit.

Michaela Morgan

Guided and Independent Writing

Collaboration

> *When I write books, I write them by myself – I couldn't bear to write in collaboration with anyone else, I'm far too jealous of my characters! With plays, it's different …We are both very egotistical and like having our own way and we each had our own ideas which we were prepared to go to any lengths to defend. At various times we both rose up and shouted angrily, 'All right, then! You can do it without me!'*
>
> *In the end, of course, it was all sorted out to our joint satisfaction and we had great fun reading the plays out loud …*

Encouraging collaboration in writing is a useful way of helping children to learn from each other. It can also provide reluctant and less confident writers with support. Peering into a creative abyss is much easier with someone by your side. However, as Jean Ure says, it is not always straightforward. Teachers need to ensure that:

- the co-authors are working together through choice

- there is not one member of the partnership who naturally dominates the other

- the children have established who is going to do what (e.g. will they plan the outline together, or each draft separate sections and then revise together?).

- there is a third party (probably you) whose advice may be sought in the event of deadlock.

Jean Ure

Create a Word Hoard!

One vital aspect of the teacher's role is to try to nurture in children that love of words which all writers share.

John Cotton

> *Then there are the words to be used in stories and poems. They call for exploration too, by looking up and noting new words encountered when reading or in conversation, discovering their histories and the way they have grown in meaning. The Old English poets used to call their vocabularies their 'Word Hoards'. I like the idea of treasure behind this, because that's what words are, a very special treasure …*

Why not learn from the poets John Cotton mentions and c reate your own Word Hoard in the classroom? Collect, display and discuss unusual, curious and fascinating words which might tempt children to use them in their writing.

The Importance of Sharing

The concept of sharing is an important one in writing – sharing experience and knowledge, sharing ideas and images and sharing to learn.

Benjamin Zephaniah

When I started writing it was only about my life, now I want to write about other people's lives, so I research by talking to people everywhere.

We share the experiences and knowledge of other people when we research what it is that we are going to write – whether it is Benjamin Zephaniah talking to the people he meets, or a child talking to an elderly person about life during the Second World War or reading about that period of history in books. Writers have experience and knowledge of so many people which they can draw upon directly and indirectly for their own work.

Through the written word, authors can reach out to readers unfettered by time, distance or even death. The images and thoughts of one brain become available to anyone.

I had lots of ideas and wanted a way of getting them out of my head so others could see them.

Tim de Jongh

It's exciting knowing that no one else in the whole world can see things in exactly the same way as I can. Making up stories in my head and then coaxing them out on paper is good.

Pratima Mitchell

We usually write for an audience other than ourselves because we want to share the ideas in our heads with other people. Every individual is unique, as Pratima Mitchell reminds us, and it is important to help children realise that their perspective – their story – is unique and special. We should do everything we can to build children's confidence and belief in themselves as writers, and helping them to understand and appreciate the unique nature of their contributions is a major step towards this.

Is it All Worth the Effort?

ANYONE can write … you don't have to be a genius! Read a lot so that you develop a feel for words, then HAVE A GO!

Judith Nicholls

One of the questions many authors ask children when they go into schools is whether or not they consider themselves to be writers. It is sad that a significant number of children do not think of themselves in this way. It is cheering, however, that in some schools virtually every child will respond positively. It proves that teachers can and do make a difference. The schools who treat children as writers and value both process and product are the schools that are likely to produce the children who relish writing and tackle it with great pride and enthusiasm.

We want children to feel the same way about their writing as the following authors feel about theirs.

The hardest part about writing is the beginning of every new book or story. The most exciting is the ending of every new book or story! The sense of achievement and of having come to know a whole new set of characters is wonderful.

Jean Ure

The most exciting things are the tingle when ideas come, when marks on the paper do magic things – wonderful!

David McKee

It's marvellous to be able to take readers or listeners into another world of my making.

Moira Andrew

The most exciting thing is when a new book comes out and people say they really like it.

Michael Rosen

I don't think any author loses the excitement of holding a new book in his or her hands for the first time.

Brian Moses

Guided and Independent Writing

C1

The Longman Book Project
© Pearson Education Ltd 2000

Ideas I Could Write About Sometime

1. The computer that tries to take over the story I am writing – changing my ideas and words if it doesn't like them.

Writing: First Draft Checklist

The Longman Book Project
© Pearson Education Ltd 2000

My checklist of things to remember
when I read my first drafts.

1. Have I missed out any important information?

C3

The Longman Book Project
© Pearson Education Ltd 2000

Borrow an Author's Ideas

These are a few of the ideas Wendy Body has in her notebook and which she may write stories about (when she has the time). Choose one of them and beat her to it! Use the back of the sheet to make some detailed notes before you do your first draft.

* In the multi-storey car park the lift's got 4 buttons marked 1, 2, 3.

The fourth one is just plain. What would happen if you pressed it? Time capsule?

* 2 good character names: Guttermuff and Rimbleglow.
G could be fantasy/animal
R sounds wizardy —
could also be a fantasy creature that glows?

* Moonsong — nice title!

* What would happen if you woke up and the sky had turned green? Especially if you were the only one who could see it? Then maybe messages start forming with clouds.

* letters in the attic
diary style written by a child for future grandchildren?

* "A cup of silver tea"

nonsense idea
but sounds like a good title

C4

The Longman Book Project
© Pearson Education Ltd 2000

Make a Storyline

Add more choices to each section below, then work with a friend to tell one of the stories.

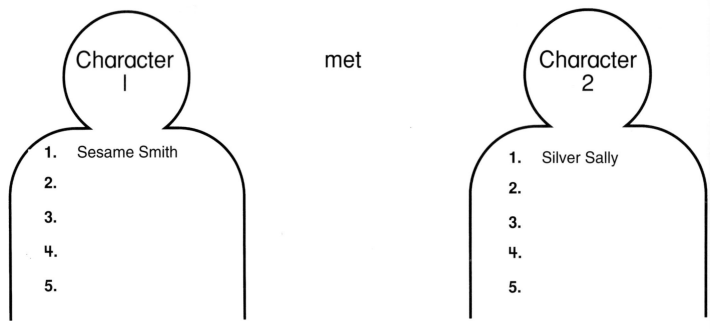

met

Character 1

1. Sesame Smith
2.
3.
4.
5.

Character 2

1. Silver Sally
2.
3.
4.
5.

and went

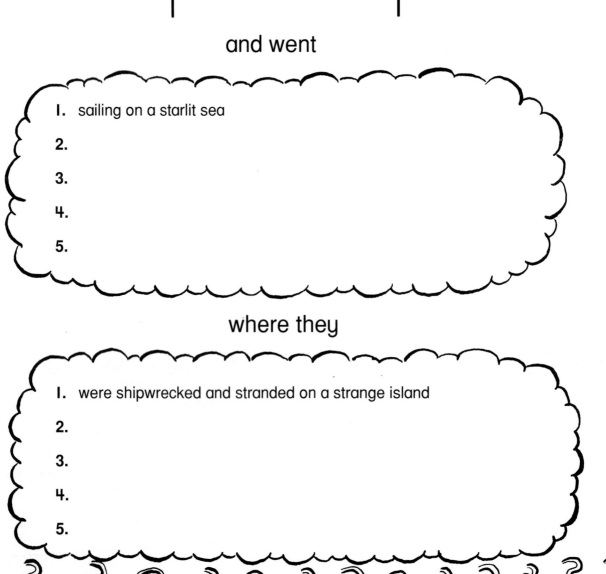

1. sailing on a starlit sea
2.
3.
4.
5.

where they

1. were shipwrecked and stranded on a strange island
2.
3.
4.
5.

C5

The Longman Book Project
© Pearson Education Ltd 2000

Words to Conjure up Characters

Read the phrases below and think about what sort of characters they conjure up in your mind. Then write a fuller description of each character.

Character A: trusting-eyed and silken-haired

Character B: weary of this world and longing for the next

Character C: eyes the colour and mood of thunder clouds

Character A

Character B

Character C

Now choose one of the characters to write a poem about.

C6

The Longman Book Project
© Pearson Education Ltd 2000

Making Things with Words

How many more different kinds of writing can you think of to add to this list?

Put a tick next to all the kinds that you have tried writing or that you use yourself.

List   **Recipe**   **Animal story**

Target to aim for:

30

How many did you get?

My Writing Record

by

I can write anywhere … I carry a notebook with me wherever I go.

Primrose Lockwood

The first thing that happens when I start writing a story is that a picture comes into my head.

Adèle Geras

Words are for weaving ideas and images, words can build worlds inside our heads to share with other people.

Wendy Body

Anything might get a poem going if you are alert … Keep awake and there are poems everywhere.

FRED SEDGWICK

I write as a way of exploring things; exploring what I've experienced, what I feel and think about things and the words I use. It is a way of looking at the world afresh …

John Cotton

Use this writing record to keep a note of the important pieces of writing that you do.
Thinking about what you have written will help you to learn from what you have done and help you to become a better writer.

What's exciting is having the idea in the first place and that lovely, crazy, scribbly stage when the ideas are tumbling onto the page – that's the best bit.

Michaela Morgan

I like to play with an idea in my head for quite some time before I begin to write. I think the idea through and try to picture settings and characters. After an initial general plan I plot each chapter. I may change things as I go along but I think the planning stage is very important.

David Webb

DATE I FINISHED THE WRITING	TITLE AND TYPE OF WRITING (STORY, PLAY, ETC.)	MY OPINION OF THIS PIECE OF WRITING

Helping Your Child With Writing – Points to Remember

Opportunities to Write

Encourage your child to do lots of real 'everyday' writing, for instance:
- informal letters to family and friends (e.g. postcards, thank-you letters, penfriends)
- formal letters (e.g. enquiries/complaints about products advertised, requests for information, letters to a local newspaper on issues which concern your child)
- notes and messages (e.g. use Post-It notes on a family bulletin board to send and receive messages from your child)
- diaries and annotated scrapbooks of special days and holidays.

Sometimes children may prefer to use a cassette recorder for some of these activities. A taped diary or 'letter' can be fun to make and helps develop skills of composition and communication.

Spelling

If your child asks you how to spell a word, either:
- help him or her look it up in the dictionary, or
- write it down.

Then ask your child to use the LOOK SAY COVER WRITE CHECK method to learn the word as he or she writes it:

LOOK   at the word carefully, and note anything special you have to remember.

SAY   the word slowly and clearly, breaking long words up into memorable parts.

COVER   the word.

WRITE   it from memory.

CHECK   to see if it's right; if not, start again.

This method should also be used for practising words for spelling homework. In this case, the process should be repeated several times for each word.

The following can be helpful in developing children's spelling skills:
- word games (e.g. *Scrabble*)
- spelling games on computer
- crosswords and wordsearches.

Vocabulary and Use of English

At this stage, it is important that children begin to use a wider range of interesting and expressive vocabulary in their writing and speech. They must also develop the use of more formal Standard English. Vocabulary and use of English is developed through:
- reading a range of good quality children's books, both fiction and non-fiction
- listening to good quality stories, plays, etc. (on cassette or radio as well as television, where the pictures can distract attention from the language)
- opportunities to talk and discuss items of interest with adults
- using a Junior Dictionary to check the meanings of unfamiliar words.

Writing for Personal Pleasure

Many children enjoy writing stories, poems and facts at home:

- Encourage your child to share what he or she has written with you.

- Praise him or her and be supportive of his or her efforts.

- Ask your child if he or she can see anything in his or her writing which could be improved or corrected rather than immediately pointing out any shortcomings or errors yourself.

- A gift of a special, attractive notebook can often inspire children to write at home! A diary as a gift also encourages children to write.

- Children and adults alike are often fascinated by family history. Encourage your child to write down what is known about your family and family anecdotes of the past and to be the scribe for recording the present.

The Longman Book Project
© Pearson Education Ltd 2000

Assessment and Record-keeping

Assessing Achievement and Progress

As well as the day-to-day informal monitoring of children's progress, it is necessary to make occasional, more detailed assessments. This is done to establish the types of reading strategies children are using and their levels of achievement with regard to National Literacy Strategy objectives. This section offers a number of copymasters to help you do this.

Child of the Day

Many teachers find the following a useful technique for giving attention to *all* the children in a class:

■ Write the names of the class members on separate index cards, and file them in a box.

■ Each day, bring forward the card at the back of the box and place it at the front. That child is the focus for special attention/observation that day.

■ It can be a day when, for example, you:
  – hear the child read for longer than usual
  – go through his/her portfolio of work
  – spend a few minutes talking about how the child sees his/her performance and progress
  – make a point of noting down any particular instructional needs/difficulties.

1 Checklists based on National Literacy Strategy Objectives

Each sheet summarises the work for the year:

C20	Technical Vocabulary Record:	Year 6
C21	Word-level Skills and Strategies Record:	Year 6
C22	Sentence-level Skills and Strategies Record:	Year 6
C23	Text-level Skills and Strategies Record:	Year 6

2 Oral Reading Behaviour and Miscue Analysis

Even though you will still be monitoring pupils' reading strategies during Guided Reading, from time to time it is sensible to take a more detailed look at how an individual child's reading is progressing – particularly those pupils who are finding reading difficult. C16 *Oral Reading Behaviour and Strategies* is intended for this purpose. There is space for the sheet to be used on six occasions to enable comparisons to be made twice a term.

Miscue analysis is a helpful technique to use when taking a detailed look at an individual child's reading. The information it provides is evidence of the strategies a child is using, misusing or not using at all. A miscue analysis summary (C17) is provided to help you do this.

When carrying out a miscue analysis:

- The child should be informed that you want him or her to try and read without help from you.

- The text should pose some degree of challenge because a text that is well within a child's competence will not offer insights as to what strategies are being used to deal with unfamiliar words.

You can either tape-record the child reading for later transcription and examination or you can:

- place a sheet of acetate over the text on your copy of the book

- mark it with a non-permanent pen while the child is reading

- transfer the information at a later stage to a miscue analysis summary (see C17).

Most teachers already have their own ways of coding children's responses. If not, the following may be used:

Miscue Analysis	**C17**

The Longman Book Project
© Pearson Education Ltd 2000

Name: .... Date: ....
Title of book: .... Pages used: ....

Errors (including self-corrections):

Number of words read: ....   Number of uncorrected errors: ....

Number of semantically appropriate substitutions/attempts: ....

Number of substitutions/attempts using phonic cues: ....

Self-corrections: ....   Non-responses: ....

Omissions: ....   Words inserted: ....

Ability to read with appropriate pace and expression:

Ability to answer questions needing a literal response:

Ability to retell episode/describe events/content:

Ability to answer questions needing an inferential or evaluative response:

Follow-up required:

Non-response/refusal:	dotted line under word
Sounding out word:	SO above word. Mark with an oblique line through the word if the child gets only part way through it
Substitution:	cross out word, write response above
Omission:	circle word the child has left out
Insertion:	add insertion mark, write extra word
Self-correction:	cross out word, write response, tick
Repetition:	underline word or phrase repeated
Pause/hesitation:	insert oblique line where pause occurs

3 Informal Assessment Sheets

Copymasters 10–15 provide assessment tasks for reading and writing. The sheets can either be clipped together to make a booklet or used separately. Children should be able to complete them with little support from you.

The tasks are designed so that they may be repeated on different occasions to allow comparison of similar pieces of work over a period of time. It is recommended that the sheets are shown to parents/guardians who may wish to comment or add information.

C10 Assessment Sheet 1: Attitudes and Preferences — Reading

C11 Assessment Sheet 2: Attitudes and Preferences — Writing

Two questionnaires, one about reading and one about writing, which children should be encouraged to answer as fully as possible.

C12 Assessment Sheet 3: Unaided Writing

Children are asked to write a minimum of 250 words about a hobby or something which really interests them.

Points for you to check: spelling, punctuation, handwriting, grammar, general presentation, cohesion and clarity of composition.

C13 Assessment Sheet 4: Understanding of Technical Vocabulary; Synonyms

Children are asked to:

■ define the meaning of ten words without using a dictionary, leaving out any which they do not know or cannot read

■ find synonyms for: *answered, big, small, attractive, nasty, ways of moving*

C14 Assessment Sheet 5: Handwriting

Children are required to copy out a sentence containing all the letters of the alphabet three times: in joined writing, capital letters and print script. They are then asked to copy a limerick or short poem in their best handwriting.

Points for you to check: correct/incorrect letter formation and joins, overall size, clear and correctly positioned ascenders and descenders which are parallel, no untoward slope to the writing. Where possible, observe children actually writing and check posture, pencil/pen grip and paper positioning in addition to the above.

C15 Assessment Sheet 6: Standard English

Children are asked to write out correctly nine sentences containing common errors.

Note: *These sheets are not intended to be a full assessment of a child's literacy skills. They offer a quick and easy-to-administer check on certain global aspects which can point the way to further, more detailed observation and assessment if there is cause for concern.*

4 Reading Certificates

Progress Certificate: Writer's Award and Progress Certificate: Achievement in Reading (C24 and C25, but unnumbered on the actual sheets) are to send home as both a pat on the back for children and as evidence of progress or effort for a child's parents/guardians.

Additional Record-keeping

The following copymasters may help to supplement/ease your record keeping.

C18 Reading Conference Record

Reading Conferences are times spent with individual children when the focus is wider than simply listening and discussing a particular book. It is a matter of choice and of time as to how frequently you see children individually. Ten to fifteen minutes every few weeks is usual.

The basic features of the Reading Conference are:

- listening to the child read a short extract and discussing the book chosen by the child

- evaluating what the child is getting/has got from the book

- seeking the child's opinion about his or her reading

- discussing what else the child has read

- making suggestions as to further reading.

The Reading Conference Record sheet provides a framework for a conference with children. You may, of course, choose not to fill in every section on each occasion.

C19 Group Reading Record (Bands 15–16)

This sheet provides an at-a-glance record of which groups have read which books and when.

The Longman Book Project
© Pearson Education Ltd 2000

Name: .... Date: ....

Circle and/or write your answers.

1. Do you like reading? A lot/Not much/A bit.

    Why?

2. What kind of books do you enjoy reading most?

3. How often do you read at home?

4. Do you think there is enough time for reading in school? Yes/No

5. What do you like/dislike about reading in school?

6. How good do you think you are at reading? How do you know?

7. Do you belong to the public library? Yes/No

    If yes, do you borrow books: very frequently/often/hardly ever?

8. What do you think would help you to become an even better reader, and why?

The Longman Book Project
© Pearson Education Ltd 2000

Name: .... Date: ....

Circle and/or write your answers.

I. Do you enjoy writing? A lot/Not much/A bit.

   Why?

2. What kind of writing do you like doing best? Why?

3. What kind of writing do you hate having to do? Why?

4. What is your opinion of the amount of writing we do in school? Is it too much, too little?

5. How would you describe your spelling?

6. How would you describe your handwriting?

7. Are there any aspects of your writing which worry you or which you find difficult?

   (e.g. writing stories)

8. Do you think you would like to earn your living as a writer one day?

The Longman Book Project
© Pearson Education Ltd 2000

Name: ....   **Date:** ....

In the space below (and on the back of the sheet if necessary), write at least 250 words about your hobby or something which really interests you.

● Do it *without* looking up any spellings or asking for help.

● Read your writing through to check for any mistakes before you hand it in.

....

by

....

The Longman Book Project
© Pearson Education Ltd 2000

Name: ....   **Date:** ....

Without using a dictionary, write the meaning of the following words.
Don't worry if there are any you don't know – go on to the next one.

Word	**Meaning**
anecdote	
asterisk	
autobiography	
biography	
footnote	
obituary	
synopsis	
proverb	
mnemonic	
narrator	

How many words can you think of with a similar meaning to
each of these words below?

answered

big

small

attractive

nasty

ways of moving

What is the longest word you can think of?

....

The Longman Book Project
© Pearson Education Ltd 2000

Name: .... **Date:** ....

1. Write out the following sentence as neatly as you can: first in joined writing, then in capital letters and then in print script.

   ## The five wizards finally kept quiet and enjoyed the boxing match.

2. Find a limerick or a short poem which you really like. Copy it out in your best handwriting and draw a decorative border round it.

The Longman Book Project
© Pearson Education Ltd 2000

Name: ....   **Date:** ....

Spot what is wrong with the following sentences and write them out correctly.

I. He never saw nothing before the car hit him.

2. Them books you give me last week weren't very good.

3. He stupidly jumped off of the bus before it had stopped.

4. The picture what she painted was hung in the hall.

5. We been out shopping with our mum and dad.

6. He was a good boy and didn't give us no trouble.

7. She asked us to do it again so this time we done it proper!

8. My friend and me decided it was the bestest film we've seen.

9. I seen her spying on what we was doing.

Oral Reading Behaviour and Strategies

Name: ....

Frequently/Yes: ✓   Rarely or never/No: ✗

On meeting unfamiliar words: Date:						
Waits to be given the word						
Attempts to work it out in some way						
Strategies for dealing with unfamiliar words:						
Haphazard guessing						
Reads on and guesses						
Re-reads and guesses						
Guesses using initial letters						
Sounds out individual letters						
Sounds out letter strings/syllables						
Looks for a known part of word						
Checks guesses for sense						
Checks guesses for visual match with word						
Other:						
Self-corrects						
Misses out words						
Misreads word endings						
Changes tense						
Responds to sentence boundaries by attending to punctuation						
Attends to punctuation within sentences						
Needs to point/mark place						
Reads in monotone						
Reads with varied expression						
Reads very slowly						
Reads very fast						

How child describes what he or she does when meeting an unknown word:

Miscue Analysis

The Longman Book Project
© Pearson Education Ltd 2000

Name: ....

Date: ....

Title of book: ....

Pages used: ....

Errors (including self-corrections):

Number of words read: ....

Number of uncorrected errors: ....

Number of semantically appropriate substitutions/attempts: ....

Number of substitutions/attempts using phonic cues: ....

Self-corrections: ....

Non-responses: ....

Omissions: ....

Words inserted: ....

Ability to read with appropriate pace and expression:

Ability to answer questions needing a literal response:

Ability to retell episode/describe events/content:

Ability to answer questions needing an inferential or evaluative response:

Follow-up required:

Reading Conference Record

C18

The Longman Book Project
© Pearson Education Ltd 2000

Name: .... **Date:** .... **Conference duration:** ....

Title of selected book: ....

Appropriate choice: Yes ☐ No ☐

Understanding of overall contents and storyline:

Performance on passage read aloud:

Child's evaluation and enjoyment of the book:

Appreciation and opinion of illustrations:

Has this book changed you or the way you think about anything?

Have you read any other books by this author? If so, what do you think of his or her writing?

Have you read any other books of this kind?

How do you feel your reading is coming along?

Book(s) recommended for further reading:

Use the reverse of this sheet for any additional comments including action suggested or taken as a result of the conference.

Group Reading Record (Bands 15–16)

C19

The Longman Book Project
© Pearson Education Ltd 2000

BAND 15						
Grandfather Singh Stories						
Quiddy and the Mysterious Mega Virus						
Through a Window						
Rich or Poor?						
Escape from Everytown						
Facing the Enemy! Classic Fiction Extracts						
BAND 16						
Myths, Legends and Monsters						
White Bird Flying						
On the Day the World Began						
Tales from the Underland						
The Quest of Isis						
Weaving Words: poems in different forms						

Technical Vocabulary: Year 6

C20

The Longman Book Project
© Pearson Education Ltd 2000

Name: ....

Date of birth : ....

Left/right handed: ....

TECHNICAL VOCABULARY	DATE CHECKED	COMMENTS
Word:		
Mnemonic		
Proverb		
Word derivation		
Sentence:		
Asterisk		
Complex sentence		
Hypothesis		
Impersonal language		
Parentheses: brackets		
commas		
dashes		
Voice: active		
passive		
Text:		
Anecdote		
Appendix, appendices		
Assonance		
Autobiography		
Biography		
Commentary		
Footnote		
Journalistic writing		
Kenning		
Limerick		
Narrator		
Obituary		
Parody		
Personification		
Riddle		
Synopsis		
Tanka		
Viewpoint		

Word-level Skills and Strategies: Year 6

C21

The Longman Book Project
© Pearson Education Ltd 2000

Name: .... **Date of birth :** ....

Left/right handed: ....

SKILLS AND STRATEGIES	DATE CHECKED	COMMENTS
Identifies misspelt words in own writing		
Keeps individual spelling log/lists		
Builds up spellings by syllabic parts, uses known prefixes, suffixes, letter strings		
Applies knowledge of rules and exceptions		
Builds words from known words and from awareness of meanings or derivations		
Uses dictionaries and computer spell-checker		
Uses visual skills, e.g. checking critical features – does it look right?		
Can spell unstressed vowels in polysyllabic words		
Can use word roots, prefixes and suffixes as a support for spelling		
Understands meaning and spelling of connectives, e.g. *therefore, furthermore, notwithstanding*		
Understands how words and expressions have changed over time, e.g. *yonder*		
Can research the origins of proper names		
Understands how new words have been added to the language		
Understands function and can use etymological dictionary		
Can invent and use spelling mnemonics		
Can explain the meaning and origins of proverbs by referring to dictionaries of proverbs and other references		
Understands that the meaning of words can change over time, e.g. *without*		
Has built a bank of useful terms and phrases for argument, e.g. *whereas*		
Has learned spelling rules and can invent own		
Can invent words using known roots, prefixes and suffixes		
Can experiment with language, e.g. creating new words, similes and metaphors		

Sentence-level Skills and Strategies: Year 6

The Longman Book Project
© Pearson Education Ltd 2000

Name: ....

Date of birth : ....

Left/right handed: ....

SKILLS AND STRATEGIES	DATE CHECKED	COMMENTS
Understands different word classes		
Understands conventions of Standard English		
Can adapt texts for particular readers and purposes		
Understands the terms active and passive, can transform one to the other and identify examples in texts		
Notes and discusses how above transformations affect word order and sense		
Investigates connecting words, phrases; collects examples from reading, etc. Studies how points are typically connected in different types of text. Classifies useful examples by position, etc. Identifies those with multiple purposes		
Can form complex sentences, e.g. using different connecting devices. Evaluates which links work best		
Understands use of: – colon – semi-colon – parenthetic commas, dashes, brackets		
Understands features of formal official language, e.g. use of impersonal voice, imperative verbs, formal vocabulary, typical words and expressions		
Can identify main clause in a sentence		
Can construct complex sentences		
Uses appropriate punctuation in above		
Can write summaries		
Can contract sentences for note-making		
Can use conditionals, e.g. if ... then		
Understands language conventions and grammatical features of texts: – narrative – recounts – instructional text – reports – explanatory text – persuasive texts – discursive texts		
Has secured control of complex sentences, understanding how clauses can be manipulated to achieve different effects		

Text-level Skills and Strategies: Year 6

The Longman Book Project
© Pearson Education Ltd 2000

Name: .... Date of birth : ....

Left/right handed: ....

SKILLS AND STRATEGIES	DATE CHECKED	COMMENTS
Can compare and evaluate print and film/TV versions of a novel or play		
Takes account of viewpoint, e.g. by identifying narrator, explaining how events might look from a different view		
Articulates responses to literature and why and how a text affects the reader		
Familiar with work of some established authors, knows what is special about their work, explains preferences in terms of authors, styles and themes		
Contributes constructively in discussion		
Can manipulate narrative perspective, e.g. by writing in voice and style of a text, writing with two different narrators		
Quickly and effectively plans plot, characters and structure of own stories		
Can summarise text in a given number of words		
Can transform section of a story into a script with stage directions, settings		
Writes poems using personification		
Revises poems for reading aloud		

Understands narrative structure, e.g.
  – how chapters/paragraphs are linked
  – how authors handle time, e.g flashback
  – how passing of time is conveyed		

Analyses how paragraphs are structured		
Recognises how poets manipulate words, e.g. for sounds, connotations, meanings		
Investigates humorous verse and appeal		
Analyses how moods, feelings, attitudes are conveyed in poetry		
Discusses, interprets challenging poems		
Identifies key features of literary texts		
Increasing familiarity with poets and writers of the past		
Uses different genres as writing models		
Can parody a literary text		
Can write summaries/commentaries crediting views, e.g. by *the writer says ...*		
Can describe and evaluate the style of an individual writer/poet		
Discusses how linked poems are related		
Comments critically on impact of a poem		
Compares, contrasts work of single writer		
Connects and contrasts the work of different writers		
Uses a reading journal effectively		
Can write a brief synopsis of a text		
Can write helpful reviews		
Can compare texts in writing, e.g. styles		
Written poems linked by theme/form		
Written extended story over period of time		

The Longman Book Project
Writer's Award
is presented to

....

for the piece of writing entitled

....

Signed: .... *Date:* ....

The Longman Book Project
© Pearson Education Ltd 2000

This Certificate is Awarded to

for Achievement in Reading

Congratulations!

Date:

Signed:

The Longman Book Project
© Pearson Education Ltd 2000

Checking Children's Reading Strategies

Children usually start learning to read by relying on:

- prior knowledge of the material being read
- words remembered from hearing the story read aloud
- a personal vocabulary of memorable words recognised on sight.

Gradually they begin to add more cueing strategies:

- use of context (which comes first)
- use of context plus initial letter cues
- as phonic knowledge and knowledge about texts increase, more sophisticated combinations of cues and checks are used.

Use of Context Cues

- When the word is well into the sentence:
  Go back to the beginning, re-read and guess.

- When the word is near the beginning of the sentence:
  Miss the word out, read on and guess.

- Always check guesses by asking:
  - *Does that make sense?*
  - *Does that sound right?*
  - *Does what you've said match the look of the word?*

- Make sure children understand *when* to re-read or to read on, i.e. it is the position of the word within the sentence that determines which strategy to use.

Use of Context plus Graphic Cues

- When re-reading or reading on and guessing a word, focus attention on the initial letter or letters:
  - *How does the word begin?*
  - *What's the sound of the first letter(s)?*

- Check guesses.

Use of Grapho-phonic Cues

- Look at the beginnings or ends of the words.
- Look for known parts within a word, e.g. *and* in *stand*, *eam* in *stream*.
- Draw attention to words which sound alike, e.g. *where: This word sounds like 'there'.*
- 'Chunk' sounds together to make the word, e.g. *scr–ee–ch > screech* or split into syllables.
- Remember that a child who cannot read a word will not be able to tell if it can be successfully 'built up' or 'sounded out' or not. If you teach this as a strategy, make sure that children understand that it will not work for all words and encourage them to use other strategies as well.
- Check by asking:
  - *Does it make sense?*
  - *Does it sound and look right?*

Children need access to a range of strategies for dealing with unfamiliar words:

- Concentrate on encouraging use of strategies which children can adopt independently and reliably when reading *without* an adult by their side. These strategies may vary from child to child.

- Children develop strategies largely as a result of the way adults prompt. If you habitually prompt in a certain way, that is the main (possibly the only) strategy children will adopt.

Use of Illustration Cues

- Looking at the illustration can occasionally help a child to predict an unfamiliar word.

- But if illustrations are detailed and complex, a child may have problems in locating the relevant part. This will distract from the reading. With longer texts, the word may not in any case be represented in the illustration.

- Discussion of illustrations before Independent Reading will add to general contextual knowledge.

Use of Self-correction

- Self-correction is a very positive sign. The child who self-corrects is the child who understands that:
  - reading has to make sense
  - words 'read' have to look right and sound right.

- Children need *time* to monitor what they have said and to amend it if necessary. Wait until the end of the sentence before saying something like: *Does that make sense?* or *Something didn't sound quite right there, did it?*

The point of reading is to recreate the author's meaning.

Children not only need praise for their efforts, they also need feedback to tell them that the strategies they are using are appropriate ones.

Four Common Reading Problems

> **I've got children who still read in a monotone – how can they be helped?**

When children are still in the process of learning to read, it is too much to expect them to monitor how they sound as well. Children do not usually realise *how* they sound when reading aloud. If a text is demanding and children are having to concentrate hard on decoding it, their expression is bound to suffer.

- Get children to record their reading on a tape recorder and then listen to it. A useful question to ask is:
  Are you reading like you talk or are you reading a bit like a robot?!

- Give children plenty of practice in reading and recording easy material – more than once if necessary – so that they can hear how much better they sound when reading with expression.

- When they are reading aloud to you, occasionally ask children to repeat a short sentence from memory and then reread it in the way they have just said it. Make a point of praising them, saying things like:
  Well done! Your voice went up and down when you read that – just like it does when you are talking or telling a story.

> **How can I best help parents/carers to support children with reading problems?**

Encourage them:

- to use paired reading:
  – adult and child read along together with the child pointing to the text to regulate the parent's/carer's speed
  – when the child feels he or she can manage some of the text alone, he or she signals this, for example by nudging the parent/carer
  – when the child meets an unknown word, the parent/carer supplies it within a few seconds and the child repeats it
  – the parent/carer reads along with the child again until the child signals.

- to give as much praise as possible and try never to lose patience with the child

- not to read with the child in front of younger brothers and sisters who are better readers.

There are a couple of children in my class who never seem to remember or even understand what it is that they are reading. What can I do?

There are some children who seem to read on 'automatic pilot' without really taking in what it is that they are reading. Check:

- that the books children are reading are not too difficult

- that there is no general circumstance which is affecting concentration and schoolwork as a whole and that a child:
  – has not got or had language problems
  – is not taking medication that will cause lack of concentration
  – is not suffering from undue lack of sleep
  – is not experiencing any emotional trauma.

When children are reading aloud, try:

- telling them before they start reading that you will stop from time to time to talk about what is happening

- asking them to stop after every page and tell you what has happened and what might happen next

- encourage parents/carers or anyone else who listens to the child reading to adopt the same strategy.

What can I do to help children who keep losing their place?

Persistent line-slipping when reading can be helped by:

- finger-pointing from *above* the line of print

- a bookmark made of thick acetate or plastic on which a line is ruled with a permanent OHP pen. This bookmark is then placed over the page with the line under the sentence being read.

Finger-pointing from below or the use of a ruler/ordinary bookmark can lead to stilted line-by-line reading because the upcoming text is hidden.

Some children are helped by putting a coloured acetate sheet over the page. Different colours (green, turquoise, blue, pink, peach, orange, yellow) appear to help different children.

■ Using the child's own interest to teach reading?
  – Ask the child to dictate a short passage (6–10 sentences) about an interest or hobby.
  – Rewrite the passage clearly on a sheet of card and write each sentence out again on separate strips of card.
  – Child matches separate sentences to full text.
  – Child sequences separate sentences correctly without full text.
  – Duplicate sentence strips. Select one pair and cut one sentence up into separate words for child to match against the complete sentence.
  – Child sequences words into correct order without full sentence.
  – Repeat with other sentences.
  – Use words to create new sentences.

■ Getting children to make their own comic-strip versions of stories enjoyed by the class?
  – Each child/pair/group can take a section of the story to work on.
  – When complete, collated, bound and displayed, these make easy readers for all the class to enjoy.

■ Making books of sounds? Children with decoding problems can be helped to make their own book of sounds or phonic elements.
  – Draw up a list of sounds the child needs to learn about, e.g.*ee, oo, ain, ight, ea, ph.*
  – Using a plain paper notebook, ask the child to head each page with one 'sound' or letter combination.
  – Help the child to think of a phrase or sentence (as funny as possible) using words containing this letter string and write it at the top of the page. For example:
    Three creepy green sheep sleeping in a jeep.
  – The child draws the picture and then gradually adds other words which fit the pattern.
  – The *All Together Now* book from *Language 1* of *The Longman Book Project* is an ideal resource for finding such words

■ Getting children to write an autobiography?
  – Write a letter to the child's parent/guardian asking if he or she
    may bring some photographs from home to make into a special
    book.
  – Use the photographs and the child's own illustrations to help him
    or her write an autobiographical account which can be made into a
    book for reading practice.
    Note: Mount the photographs with proper mounts so that the
    pictures can be safely removed and returned to parents later.

Identifying Special Needs

Many learning difficulties have underlying physical or developmental causes. If you suspect that children have any of the difficulties outlined below, the first action should be to consult their parents.

Language impairment

Look out for the child who has particular difficulty in:
- articulating sounds and pronouncing words
- understanding words, sentences or ideas
- comprehending written text
- following instructions
- learning new words and accessing the right word
- conveying meaning through words
- using language appropriately in various contexts.

Specialist help
Refer to speech therapist.

General pointers for teaching
- Keep instructions short and clear.
- Begin instructions with the child's name.
- Repeat instructions.
- Check child's understanding by asking him or her to repeat or explain instructions.
- Create opportunities for purposeful, focused talk (with adults or other children).
- Use time with the child to reinforce key vocabulary.

Motor control problems

Look out for the child who shows greater than average:
- general clumsiness
- coordination difficulties (e.g. in P.E.)
- poor hand or finger control (e.g. unable to hold pencil or scissors).

Specialist help
Refer to school doctor.

General pointers for teaching
- Use clear language for instructions.
- Stress spatial relationships, position and direction.
- Demonstrate and develop child's large-scale motor control (big movements like sky-writing and painting) before small-scale activities like handwriting.
- Let child sometimes practise on the board or at a large easel.
- Allow child to dictate some written work to you or a classroom helper whenever possible.
- When child is writing for him or herself:
  – see if commercial pencil grips are helpful
  – provide a sloping desk rather than a flat one
  – encourage the use of a word-processing package on the computer.

Visual impairment

Look out for the child who:

- holds a book at a particular distance from his or her eyes
- holds a book at an unusual angle, or angles his or her head oddly
- frequently rubs his or her eyes
- screws up or half-closes his or her eyes when reading
- does not like bright (or dim) light
- has frequent headaches or feels dizzy.

Specialist help

Refer to optician or school doctor (ask about possible referral to an orthoptist).

General pointers for teaching

- If the child has glasses, ensure that they are worn when necessary and kept clean.
- Make sure child has a clear view of the board and any other focus of teaching.
- Ensure the lighting where the child sits suits his or her needs as well as possible (good diffuse lighting that does not cause glare from the page is preferable).
- Some children may be helped by coloured lenses or overlays.

Hearing impairment (including intermittent hearing loss)

Look out for the child who:

- has frequent colds, earache or catarrh
- speaks unclearly
- misinterprets verbal instructions
- does not respond when he or she cannot see the teacher's face
- looks carefully at the teacher's face (in order to lip-read)
- varies in his or her performance in school (as deafness comes and goes)
- seems confused and unable to participate in noisy discussions and activities.

Specialist help

Refer to school doctor or peripatetic teacher for the hearing-impaired.

General pointers for teaching

- Face the child when speaking to him or her.
- Keep background noise as low as possible, or bear its effects in mind.
- Speak clearly to the child when giving instructions, and repeat instructions if necessary.
- Ask child to repeat or explain instructions to check understanding.

Specific learning difficulties (dyslexia)

Children of seven or over who have unexpected or unaccountable difficulties with reading and/or writing may have a specific learning difficulty, sometimes known as dyslexia.

Look out for the child who has problems in more than one of the following areas:

- writes numbers or letters back to front, e.g. *b/d p/q*
- reverses the order of numerals or letters in words, e.g. *51* for *15*, *si* for *is*
- makes bizarre spelling mistakes
- in maths, uses bricks, fingers or marks on paper to help with counting
- has difficulty in telling left from right
- has particular difficulty learning to tell the time
- has difficulty with sequences, e.g. months of the year, the alphabet.

Specialist help

Refer to an educational psychologist for assessment. Seek advice from local SEN service.

General pointers for teaching

- Give as much extra help with reading as possible on a one-to-one basis.
- Don't ask the child to read aloud in front of others (unless he or she wants to).
- Make sure he or she understands any written instructions in maths workbooks, etc.
- If the child has severe difficulties with writing, try to provide a scribe for some written work.
- Encourage use of the computer/word processor (look for programmes designed for dyslexic children).
- Provide a tables square and don't expect the child to learn tables.
- Encourage the child's parent/carer to read to him or her as much as possible.
- Use paired and Shared Reading techniques.
- Try not to be over-critical about 'careless' mistakes or untidiness, and accentuate the positive aspects of the child's work.

Grandfather Singh Stories

Author: *Pratima Mitchell*

Illustrator: *Marie Corner*

Genre: *three realistic stories told in the first person*

Whole Class Work

Shared Text Extract (Pack 11)

Grandfather must be the most popular man on our side of town. He knows everybody and tries to help everyone in all kinds of ways. He'll look after Jenny next-door's baby, or come into school to fix a broken door or mend the sink. Or if Mr Patel has to go to the dentist, Grandfather is called upon to mind Lovely Department Store (it's only a midget corner shop) and he always says yes.

You see him all over the place, all six feet of him; and his bright turban gives him even greater height. He marches rather than walks, swinging his long arms as if he's on a parade ground. Before he came to England with my granny, he was in the army and after that he was a master carpenter. Now he's retired and spends almost all his time on his allotment.

There's a whole colony of these allotment freaks down there. Some of them are his friends but one or two of the freaks enjoy being poisonously unfriendly. There's a lot of jealousy about who grows the biggest marrows and onions and bags first prize in the South Eastern Allotment Growers' Co-operative Annual Fruit, Vegetable and Flower Show. Mr Khruschev and Mr Porcini will do almost anything to sabotage their rivals and Grandfather is definitely Rival Number One.

Shared Reading

- What evidence does the text provide to back up the statement: *Grandfather must be the most popular man on our side of town?*

- What evidence does the text provide which indicates that Grandfather is a helpful and thoughtful person?

- What does the phrase *allotment freaks* mean? Is it the kind of phrase which Grandfather himself might use? Why?

- Why might Grandfather be *Rival Number One* as far as Mr Khruschev and Mr Porcini are concerned?

- How would children describe the general tone of the extract and the narrator's viewpoint? Affectionate? Objective?

Shared Writing Activity Page

Writing in the style of the extract.

- What makes this a successful character description?

- Write a character study of Grandmother in the style of the extract.

Other Shared Writing Ideas

Write a letter of recommendation to support a proposal to give Grandfather an award for services to the community.

Word- and Sentence-level Work

- List and define less familiar words and phrases such as *master carpenter, sabotage, Co-operative, parade ground.*

- Discuss the use of brackets to indicate an aside in the first paragraph.

- Identify the simpler, shorter sentences. Model how to make them into complex sentences.

- Identify complex sentences and other ways of making them complex, e.g. using participles.

Guided and Independent Work

Text-level Work

- Consider the structure of the book by looking at the chapter headings first. What kind of stories do the children think these will be?

- Discuss how Grandfather would be described by different characters in the book, e.g. his grandchildren, wife, Mr Porcini, Mr Krushchev.

- Identify the narrator by reading page 3. Discuss the first person point of view and how you can identify this in writing – 'I'.

- List some of the advantages and disadvantages of having a first person narrator, e.g. can you trust what they say?

- Discuss the chatty style of the book and its appropriateness to the character of the narrator. Would children identify with more formal language?

- Are these stories mainly funny, sad, exciting or all three? What makes them so?

Guided Writing Ideas

Write a version of page 3 as a third person narrator and compare both versions. What changes are required in the pronouns and tenses?

Sentence-level Work

- Use *There's* on page 39 to revise agreement of nouns and verbs, i.e. *there is a ghost ... there are ghosts.*

- Discuss Standard English and the appropriateness of style to the audience in the light of slang in the book, e.g. page 48. In which situations is slang appropriate?

- Collect specialist vocabulary, e.g. gardening words from page 29: *seedlings, crop, insecticide, allotment.*

- Consider the difference between commas and semi-colons in lists on page 9 – to separate clauses and to separate larger lists. You may also like to consider the function of the brackets on this page.

Word-level Work

- Collect words from other cultures, e.g. page 64. How can the children find out what these words mean if they are not in a dictionary? Consider how the pictures in the book can help.

- List any new words arising from slang usage, e.g. *veggie* (page 28); *loo* (page 48). Discuss how words which were once slang, e.g. *bus* as an abbreviation of *omnibus*, are now Standard English.

- Revise inflectional endings, e.g. *special, precious* (page 29); *competition* (page 28). Break the words into syllables.

- Look again at unstressed vowels in polysyllabic words, e.g. page 43, *independent, sometimes, favourite*. Circle vowels which often get missed out.

Independent Work

- Make a dictionary of words from other countries, providing suitable definitions.

- List connectives, e.g. *nevertheless, therefore,* and break them into syllables to spell.

- Give children simple sentences and ask them to make them into complex ones using a series of connectives.

- Experiment with changing the simple sentences using participles, e.g. *making ...*

Plenary

- Assess and monitor children's awareness of sentences and sentence structure by discussing their sentences using connectives and participles.

- Read some definitions in the dictionaries and ask children to guess the words.

- Ask children to add other words they know and their meanings.

Copymasters

C1 Making and supporting statements about character

C2 Investigating proverbs

Quiddy and the Mysterious Mega Virus

Author: *Alison Leonard*

Illustrator: *Harriet Dell*

Genre: *adventure/mystery; strong character interest involving disability*

Whole Class Work

Shared Text Extract (Pack 11)

Meanwhile, at Geoffrey's house, Geoffrey's mother was on the telephone. The surgery receptionist thought she was hysterical and wouldn't let her talk to the doctor.

"But I must speak to him personally!" she insisted.

"Last week my little boy had the flu. Now it's turned to pneumonia!"

Geoffrey, behind her, was spluttering with fury and embarrassment.

"Mum!" he said. "I didn't have flu, I haven't got pneumonia now and I don't need the doctor! It's a sort of computer virus, not a flu one. It doesn't give us all a temperature, it makes us ..."

The receptionist had gone away to consult her colleagues, so Geoffrey's mother turned for a moment to listen to what Geoffrey was saying.

"Makes you do what?"

"Say stupid sentences, shout shocking sayings. Alliterate alphabetically. Fabricate fancy fables. Produce potty paroxysms." Geoffrey was beginning to enjoy himself. "Gaily gush gossip. Twitter tongue-wagging tittle-tattle –"

"Stop!" wailed Mrs Cosford. "Doctor – is that you? Fetch an ambulance at once – my son is in a state of complete kleptomaniac collapse!"

Geoffrey said as she put the phone down, "Kleptomaniac starts with a 'k'. And it means stealing things. I haven't got kleptomania – what I've got is verbal diarrhoea."

"Diarrhoea, as well! Oh – will this monster ever go back to being my own sweet Geoffrey again?"

Shared Reading

- Ensure the children have read or heard up to page 66. Establish the main and supporting characters and retell the story so far.

- Read the shared extract. Consider the way the story moves from one event to another and explore how the three passages are linked.

- Consider the implications of the virus for Clara and Quiddy. Identify and discuss their unspoken concerns.

- Look at Mrs Cosford's reaction, and decide whether her response is reasonable in the circumstances, citing examples in the text to support opinions.

Shared Writing Activity Page

Plan a fantasy story where something makes people behave out of character. Headings given: *Setting, Characters, Initiating Event/Problem, Episodes, Resolution, Possible titles.*

Other Shared Writing Ideas

Rewrite some of the dialogue as reported speech

Word- and Sentence-level Work

- Collect specialist words related to Geoffrey's supposed illness, e.g. *temperature, pneumonia.* Point out that *flu* is a diminutive of *influenza.* Why is *kleptomania* wrong in this context?

- Explore Mrs Cosford's confusion with the word *virus.* Identify other homonyms that could be confusing, e.g. *post, wave.*

- *Geoffrey was beginning to enjoy himself.* Look at how alliteration in advertising and poetry can be enjoyable.

- Explore Geoffrey's changing tense in his explanation to his mother.

Guided and Independent Work

Text-level Work

- Discuss the description of Quiddy on page 3 and what makes her special.

- What are the children's reactions to having a person with a disability as the central character of a story?

- What image of disability does the book promote?

- Read some of the captions which introduce the chapters and predict what these will be about.

- Is it a surprise when Quiddy realises that Patrick is the cause of the virus or did children already suspect this? If so, when did they begin to think this and why?

- Read the last page to find out what *Quiddy* means. Investigate and collect other names with meanings, and names which are also homonyms, e.g. *Mark*.

Guided Writing Ideas

- Experiment with writing stories in speech bubbles. What are the advantages and disadvantages?

- Rewrite a section of the story as a news report or television bulletin.

Sentence-level Work

- Discuss differences in verb, person, etc. between the speech bubbles and the narration.

- Identify the different tenses of verb on page 31 and discuss their use, e.g. *shall, could, are.*

- Formal vocabulary and usage can be identified and discussed by considering the words of the Queen and the Members of Parliament, e.g. page 120.

- Pinpoint examples of dashes, colons and brackets on page 82 and identify their functions.

- Experiment with isolating the main clause in a complex sentence, checking that it will stand on its own, e.g. the top two lines of page 61.

Word-level Work

- Identify specialist computer language and acronyms, such as on page 52.

- Discuss new words in the language, e.g. *robot* (page 123), and how old words, e.g. *virus,* can attain a new meaning.

- Look at how the book plays with language, e.g. on page 67.

- Consider acronyms on page 50. Generate other examples.

- Read the collection of idiomatic phrases, used on page 122, and ascertain their meaning. Brainstorm others the children may know to add to the collection.

- Revise investigation of unstressed vowels in polysyllabic words, as in *important, interested* and *ordinary* on page 78.

Independent Work

- Think about a time when Clara may have to leave Quiddy. Write their thought bubbles.

- Collect and illustrate confusing homonyms, clarifying the definition of each one.

- Write funny alliterative phrases to advertise yourself or your best friend.

- Write a description of the relationship between Clara and Quiddy and how it develops.

- Arthur King is captured and put on trial for treason. Plan and present the evidence for the prosecution and the defence. What will the verdict and sentence be?

Plenary

- Consider how effective the alliterative adverts were. How does humour help advertising? Collect examples from the media.

- Compare and contrast some of the descriptions of the relationship between Clara and Quiddy.

Copymasters

C4 Questions and characterisation

C5 Making a crossword

Through a Window

Author: *selected by Wendy Body*

Illustrator: *photographs*

Genre: *poetry anthology with poems of differing length, form and mood written by women*

Whole Class Work

Shared Text Extract (Pack 11)

Jack's Tale
by Judith Nicholls

"At day-break, Jack finding the Giant not likely to be soon roused, crept softly out of his hiding-place, seized the hen, and ran off with her,"
(Iona and Peter Opie: The Classic Fairy Tales)

Sun rises before me,
dazzles pathless flight.
In the corner of each eye
mists drift and fade,
dissolve against a lightening sky;
the tops of oaks sprawl
like giant undergrowth below,
I dare not pause to gaze,
I dare not fall!

Behind, as if in smoke,
the castle disappears.

My life is ruled by noise:
heart drums inside my chest,
the giant thud of angry steps
invades my ears.

Beneath one arm
a squirming weight of feathers,
crooked between waist and elbow,
squawks our whereabouts into the dawn;
scratches tales of panic into flesh.
All thoughts are on escape:
all golden dreams have flown!
Ahead, at last,
green stalks emerge from cloud
then cobweb downwards,
stitching earth to sky.
I leap, grasp branches urgently
with outstretched hand: half-slide, half-fall
to blessed earth below,
to blessed land.

Shared Reading

- Before reading the extract, ask the children to retell the story of *Jack and the Beanstalk.*

- Read both parts of the text. Discuss why the poet felt she should include the passage from the fairy tale.

- Why are some lines written in italic font?

- Pose five questions that could be asked about this poem and show how words and phrases in the text can provide the answers.

Shared Writing Activity Page

Imagery.

Discuss what the poet is describing. Write alternative descriptions using similes and metaphors. For example:
green stalks emerge from cloud
then cobweb downwards,
stitching earth to sky.

Other Shared Writing Ideas:

Start another narrative poem based on a traditional story, e.g. *Red Riding Hood,* written in the first person.

Word- and Sentence-level Work

- Consider the use of the present tense and how this builds suspense.

- Explore transforming the auxiliary verb *dare* and discuss whether the poet's choice is the most effective.

- Consider the use of semi-colons, colons and commas and their function in the text, e.g. to separate clauses.

- Identify and discuss examples of figurative language.

- What other typography could be used to create effect, e.g. words in bold, capitalisation?

Guided and Independent Work

Text-level Work

- Read the introduction. Find an example of each of the three types of poem mentioned in lines 3 and 4. Explain the reasons for choices.

- Compare and contrast the two poems about people who have no homes: 'Pearlie Mountblossom' and 'Nursery Rhyme 1992', in terms of theme, form and central characters.

- Choose two poems with different moods and examine how the poet creates the mood/atmosphere.

- Read the poem on page 32. Discuss what aspects of the boy's remark made a poem. Can you expand on it?

- How well do the photographs fit or interpret the poems which they accompany?

Guided Writing Ideas

Use the poem 'February' as a model for poems about other months.

Sentence-level Work

- Investigate the use of punctuation in the poems. How might poems such as 'Pete's Leg' or 'Shadow' have been punctuated had the poet decided to do so?

- Read the poems on pages 31 and 32. Find an example of a simile and a metaphor.

- Consider the passing of time in 'School Reports' (page 36). Add a conjunction, e.g. *but, additionally, however,* to the end of each verse to expand on what the teacher is implying.

- Experiment with expanding the short lines in 'I Don't Cry' (page 24) into fuller, more complex sentences. How does this alter the impact of the poem?

Word-level Work

- Identify the onomatopoeic words in 'Family Meals'. Add other examples.

- List any unfamiliar words, predict meaning from context and check with a dictionary. Compile a glossary to go with the book.

- Write your own examples of simile and metaphors to describe the night, based on 'Night' (page 31).

- Look at the words *translucencies* on page 26. Generate a definition based on the evidence in the text and related to knowledge of syllabic parts.

- Identify words in 'Wheels-Song' that indicate its contemporary setting, e.g. *trainers, ghettoblaster*. Read the other poems. Are they all contemporary? Find evidence in the texts.

Independent Work

- Write Jack's retelling of his adventure to his mother. Note the tense changes required. How would Jack embellish his tale? Compare this with the giant's version of the event to his wife and then write that.

- Complete the narrative poem started in Shared Writing.

- Select a favourite poem and prepare it for performance.

Plenary

- Compare Jack's and the giant's retelling and consider the differences in language and point of view.

- Read other versions of the same event. Compare linguistic features (powerful verbs, tense, contracted sentences), used to describe Jack's rush down the beanstalk.

Copymasters

C7 Choosing lines with effective word use

C8 Finding examples of language features

Rich or Poor?

Author: *Pratima Mitchell*
Illustrator: *Jane Tattersfield*
Genre: *retelling of 12 Indian folk-tales with introduction*

Whole Class Work

Shared Text Extract (Pack 11)

Surajmal's Journey to Heaven

Once upon a time, a king of India had a minister who was a jewel without price. His name was Ajit Singh and he was wise, honest, learned and clever. He knew all about money and taxes, all about war and farming; and he had the art of making people happy. Moreover, he was handsome, tall and strong with a magnificent moustache and piercing eyes. He could ride and hunt expertly and was an archer beyond compare. Of course his wife was lovely and charming and his children delightful and well-mannered. He had everything, especially the friendship and support of the king.

But in the wings of his happy and successful life, a green-eyed monster was lurking, waiting to pounce on Ajit Singh. A group of the king's courtiers became more and more jealous of this favoured minister. One of them, Surajmal, started to poison the king's mind against Ajit Singh.

"I've heard," said the wicked Surajmal, "that Ajit Singh's head is getting bigger than a pumpkin. He thinks that he can do anything at all in the world. I've even heard him say," the liar whispered, "that he's better at everything than your majesty."

It was a pity that the king bothered to listen to such rubbish, but he did and he was peeved.

Shared Reading

- Before reading the extract, read the author's introduction on page 5. What does this lead the reader to expect of the stories to come?

- From the chapter's title, predict the traditional story elements that might be included.

- Read the extract. Consider how the author might be trying to influence the reader's view.

- How does Ajit Singh fit the mould of a traditional story character?

- What conclusions can we draw as to the king's character – is he a strong or weak personality?

- Discuss possible outcomes for the story.

Shared Writing Activity Page

Metaphors and similes.

This is how the author describes Surajmal's jealousy of Ajit Singh using metaphor and personification: *But in the wings of his happy and successful life, a green-eyed monster was lurking, waiting to pounce.*

How could the following emotions be described: *anger, fear, cowardice, sorrow, joy?*

Other Shared Writing Ideas

Extend the conversation between Surajmal and the king.

Word- and Sentence-level Work

- What is the *green-eyed monster*? Look for the definition in the text. Brainstorm other descriptions for emotions, particularly the way colours are used.

- Consider the meaning of phrases, such as *in the wings* and *pressed home the point.*

- Summarise the extract in three points.

- Invent and define new words to describe the characters in the extract, using known syllabic parts, e.g. *magnifisome,* as a description of Ajit Singh.

Guided and Independent Work

Text-level Work

- Read the first paragraph on page 9. Is the author trying to influence the reader's perception of Akbar? How?

- Use the story 'The Most Sacred Day of the Year' (pages 47-50) to identify the different points of view of the characters.

- Explore how the author denotes the passage of time in 'Sheemant and the Goddess Chandi' (pages 71-75).

- Read the opening paragraphs of each story. What common features does the author employ to capture the reader's attention?

- 'Rich or poor' may not always refer to material wealth. Discuss who is really rich and who is really poor in each of these stories?

Guided Writing Ideas

Read the author's introduction (pages 5–7) in which she explains some of the features in the stories. Summarise this information into one paragraph that could be used as a back cover blurb for the book.

Sentence-level Work

- Explore the use of passive verbs on page 48 (paragraphs 2 and 3).

- Look for examples of formal language, e.g. on pages 38–39. Consider the reasons why this style of language is being used.

- Read 'The Golden Rat' (pages 17–21). Summarise, in note form, the events that led to Madan becoming a rich man.

- Look at the last two paragraphs on page 64 to secure understanding of commas in complex sentences and punctuation to indicate speech passages.

- Read the saying from the Buddhist scriptures on page 57. Use this to initiate study of proverbs and sayings with similar meanings, and from various sources.

Word-level Work

- To what is the 'green-eyed monster' on page 65 referring? Explore how other human emotions are described in stories.

- Use compound words such as *disobedience* (page 32) and *conversationally* (page 53) to experiment with building new words from known syllabic parts.

- Look at *geometric* (page 29) to revise work on technical words from Year 5. Investigate and collect words families, such as *geography* and *symmetrical*.

- Use the second and third paragraphs on page 53 to consolidate the children's knowledge and spelling of prefixes and suffixes, such as *un, tion, ic, able*.

Independent Work

- Write three alternative endings for *Surajmal's Journey to Heaven*, giving reasons for the predictions.

- Define and illustrate invented words.

- Take the plot of any one of the stories. See if it has a moral and retell it, bringing it up to date with modern characters and settings.

- Most of these stories have clearly signalled villains. Who is the most evil? Is the punishment received in the story appropriate? Why?

Plenary

- Consider the endings. Are they feasible? Read on in the story to assess their success.

- Compare and contrast the children's views of the villains and their punishment.

Copymasters

C10 Questions about the book

C11 Identifying and writing conditional sentences

Escape from Everytown

Author: *Terrance Dicks*

Illustrator: *Chris Priestley*

Genre: *humorous fantasy adventure, which includes episodes based on classic novels*

Whole Class Work

Shared Text Extract 1 (Pack 11)

One by one they gave their names and addresses. The Guardian wrote them all down in a big leather-covered book, using a steel-nibbed, wooden pen dipped into a metal inkwell.

"Haven't you got a computer?" asked Arnie.

"Yes," said the Guardian. She tapped her forehead. "In here!" She pointed up the stairs. "Up there you will find the Stacks. You may each choose one book to borrow for one week."

"Aren't books a bit old-fashioned?" asked Arnie.

"Nonsense. A book is a highly complex communication device, involving time travel, telepathy and life after death. It puts you in direct mental communication with the mind of the writer, even if that writer died hundreds of years ago!" The Guardian looked round the group. "Before you go on, I must warn you!"

"What about?" asked Arnie nervously.

"Just now you said you weren't afraid of books. Well, you should be! Books are the most wonderful and terrible things in the world. They can change lives, change history even. If you go up there, you may never be the same again. So, if you are afraid, turn back now, and rejoin the ranks of the empty-headed." The Guardian sighed. "Don't worry, you'll be in the majority."

By now Kim was convinced that the Guardian was crazy, but she wasn't gong to refuse a challenge. Empty-headed indeed! "We'll go up," she said. "Won't we?"

Shared Reading

- Introduce the extract by telling children that the book is set in the future at a time when technological advances mean that children do not read books and libraries are very rare. The characters have just discovered one.

- Who is the Guardian? Why is she so named? Why doesn't Terrance Dicks call her a librarian?

- What does the Guardian mean when she says that books involve *time travel, telepathy and life after death*?

- What might the Guardian's view of modern technology be? What evidence is there in the extract to suggest this?

Shared Writing Activity Page

Writing a Descriptive Summary.

The writer says that: *A book is a highly complex communication device, involving time travel, telepathy and life after death ...*

How would you describe books and their power to children in the future who are only used to computer screens?

Other Shared Writing Ideas

Write a set of instructions on how to use a library.

Word- and Sentence-level Work

- Identify and discuss the examples of hyphenated words *(leather-covered, steel-nibbed, old-fashioned, empty-headed)*.

- Identify the main clauses in sentences and then use a non-permanent pen to underline them.

- Identify and discuss use of conditionals, e.g. *if you are afraid, turn back now*

- Investigate the origins of *telepathy* and other words with this prefix.

The Guardian's words seemed to echo in all their minds. Somewhere ahead their books were waiting for them.

Amy found herself in a quiet alcove. She stretched out her hand and a book seemed almost to float into it. Its brightly coloured cover showed a dark girl in a long white dress, clasped in the arms of a handsome soldier. "Some trashy romance," thought Amy disapprovingly. She opened the book ...

She was the girl in the white dress, covered now by a travelling-cloak, and she was hurrying along cobbled streets. From somewhere in the distance came the rumble of gunfire. The street was full of little groups of people, talking uneasily.

Not far away, near a little village called Waterloo, a great battle was being fought – and no one yet knew who had won or lost. Brussels was filled with all kinds of rumours. Some said that the English had already lost, pointing out that Napoleon, the great French leader, had never really been defeated.

A line of carts swung around the corner, each one filled with weary, mud-covered men – rough, blood-soaked bandages around terrible wounds. Their faces were haggard and pale, but they tried to smile and look cheerful. One or two waved feebly at the onlookers. Some called feebly for water. Most just lay there, too weak and dazed to move.

English wounded brought back from the battlefield. "Perhaps we've lost after all," she thought.

Shared Reading

- Read the third paragraph of the extract. What does it tell us, indirectly, about the setting? (Perhaps it is wartime?)

- What clues tell us the period and place in which the extract is set?

- Who is fighting whom in the battle? How do we know? Which facts give the impression that the English are losing?

- What has actually happened to Amy?

- Read individual paragraphs of the text, practising use of natural expression to maintain the listener's interest.

Shared Writing Activity Page

Experiment with different ways of punctuating the extract:

Not far away near a little village called waterloo a great battle was being fought and no one yet knew who had won or lost brussels was filled with all kinds of rumours some said that the english had already lost pointing out that napoleon the great french leader had never really been defeated a line of carts swung around the corner each one filled with weary mud covered men rough blood soaked bandages around terrible wounds

Other Shared Writing Ideas

Rewrite the final six sentences, experimenting with different ways of combining them.

Word- and Sentence-level Work

- Revise spelling patterns for words with unstressed vowels (e.g. *soldier*).

- Re-express some of the complex sentences in a different order (e.g. *Some said that the English...*); rewrite others in shorter, simple sentences.

- Look at the use of the past perfect (to refer to another time, further back in the past). Transform sentences into other tenses.

- Identify and discuss the examples of hyphenated words (*travelling-cloak, mud-covered, blood-soaked*). Distinguish between hyphens and dashes.

Guided and Independent Work

Text-level Work

- Identify the classic novels used within this fantasy text.

- Investigate and discuss the linking of chapters and episodes.

- Discuss the effect that the books have on the characters.

- Compile a list of titles of books to help people, e.g. a book on overcoming fear (*The 18th Emergency*?) to help a timid person.

- Re-read page 17. Discuss and then write your own views on the power of books and reading.

- Identify the key features of different types of literary text, e.g. characters, (pages 28–29, 32–36, 36–38, 46–47, 48–55, 56–69, 70–80).

- What might Terrance Dicks's purpose have been in writing this book?

Guided Writing Ideas

Compose a persuasive text in favour of reading.

Sentence-level Work

- Ask children to select examples of long, complex sentences for group discussion and identification of main clauses.

- Rewrite long sentences as shorter ones.

- Construct one sentence from shorter ones, discussing and using appropriate connectives.

- Read or listen to sentences and decide whether the setting is Old Town or Everytown. Discuss how we can tell (e.g. technology versus descriptions of life without it).

- Find sentences that describe physical violence with imagery, e.g. on page 59. Use them as a model for writing your own sentences.

- Revise the use of punctuation conventions for speech, e.g. page 36.

Word-level Work

- Set the task of finding ten words which have a suffix and ten words which have a prefix, e.g. *disappeared, unexpectedly* (page 43).

- List any words which are unfamiliar while reading. Check meanings after reading.

- Collect examples of words and expressions that show that the book is set in the future, e.g. *vidiphone* (page 30).

- Use page 38 (paragraphs 1 and 2) as a cloze activity for exploring endings for the verb *worry*.

- Find examples of words with multiple meanings, e.g. 'the Indian *band* ' (page 57) and investigate the alternatives. From the context, explain what it is that helps us find the right meaning.

Independent Work

- Make a list of words that can function as both a noun and a verb. Write examples (e.g. *swing, bandage, scuttle, face, flock*) of both uses in sentences.

- Collect and classify *ou* words to revise spelling and pronunciation rules. Add to lists.

- Write a paragraph for each of the children in the book which summarises how and why they are changed by their experiences.

- Given a style, setting and plot, write your own extract from a book.

Plenary

- Review and assess the children's ability to transform the tense of a sentence, by asking them to change sentences from the text.

- Sample and discuss the children's summary paragraphs. Is there agreement on how the characters changed?

Copymasters

C12 Questions about the book

C13 Making complex sentences

Facing the Enemy!

Author: *selected by Wendy Body*
Illustrators: *Sarah Warburton and Colin Howard*
Genre: *extracts from classic novels linked by theme*

Whole Class Work

Shared Text Extract 1 (Pack 10)

**From *Oliver Twist*
by *Charles Dickens***

Crimson with fury, Oliver started up, overthrew the chair and table; seized Noah by the throat; shook him in the violence of his rage, till his teeth chattered in his head; and, collecting his whole force into one heavy blow, felled him to the ground.

A minute ago, the boy had looked the quiet, mild, dejected creature that harsh treatment had made him. But his spirit was roused at last; the cruel insult to his dead mother had set his blood on fire. His breast heaved; his attitude was erect; his eye bright and vivid; his whole person changed, as he stood glaring over the cowardly tormentor who now lay crouching at his feet; and defied him with an energy he had never known before.

"He'll murder me!" blubbered Noah. "Charlotte! missis! Here's the new boy a murdering of me! Help! help! Oliver's gone mad! Char - lotte!"

Noah's shouts were responded to, by a loud scream from Charlotte, and a louder from Mrs Sowerberry; the former of whom rushed into the kitchen by a side-door, while the latter paused on the staircase till she was quite certain that it was consistent with the preservation of human life, to come farther down.

"Oh, you little wretch!" screamed Charlotte, seizing Oliver with her utmost force, which was about equal to that of a moderately strong man in particularly good training.

Shared Reading

- Why is Oliver in a rage?

- How do we know that this behaviour is out of character? Underline the parts of the text which are evidence.

- Does the extract contain any examples of humorous writing? What makes them so? Understatement? Exaggeration?

- What does *it was consistent with the preservation of human life, to come farther down* mean? What could the author have said instead? Would it be less effective?

Shared Writing Activity Page

Writing a summary.

- Write a summary of the extract using about 60 words.

- Write another summary using no more than 20 words.

Other Shared Writing Ideas

Write the dialogue between Noah and Mr Sowerberry in which Noah explains what happened and why.

Word- and Sentence-level Work

- Identify and investigate the numerous examples of Dickens' use of semi-colons. What other ways of punctuating these sentences might be possible?

- *Here's the new boy a murdering of me!* Is this sentence in Standard English? Why is it written like this?

- Explain the meanings and find alternatives for: *dejected, his attitude was erect, his spirit was roused at last.*

**From *The Hobbit*
by J. R. R. Tolkien**

At that moment Bilbo threw. The stone struck the spider plunk on the head, and it dropped senseless off the tree, flop to the ground, with all its legs curled up.

The next stone went whizzing through a big web, snapping its cords, and taking off the spider sitting in the middle of it, whack, dead. After that there was a deal of commotion in the spider-colony, and they forgot the dwarves for a bit, I can tell you. They could not see Bilbo, but they could make a good guess at the direction from which the stones were coming.

As quick as lightning they came running and swinging towards the hobbit, flinging out their long threads in all directions, till the air seemed full of waving snares.

Bilbo, however, soon slipped away to a different place. The idea came to him to lead the furious spiders further and further away from the dwarves, if he could; to make them curious and angry all at once. When about fifty had gone off to the place where he had stood before, he threw some more stones at these, and at others that had stopped behind; then dancing among the trees he began to sing a song to infuriate them and bring them all after him, and also to let the dwarves hear his voice.

Shared Reading

- Establish that Bilbo is trying to rescue his companions, the dwarves, from the clutches of the giant spiders.

- Does Bilbo have more than one purpose in attacking the spiders in this way? If so, what are they? (To kill/disable the spiders because he hates/fears them? To lead them away from the dwarves? To rescue his companions?) Or is it the case that the first two are the means of achieving a single purpose?

- How would children describe the mood and tone of the extract?

- *I can tell you.* To whom does this refer? Discuss the effect of such stylistic devices and their purpose of appealing directly to the reader in an attempt to draw him/her into the story.

Shared Writing Activity Page

Poetry writing.

Finish the words to the song which Bilbo might have sung to make the spiders *curious and angry all at once*.

Other Shared Writing Ideas

- Write a brief synopsis of the text for a back cover blurb.

- Write a commentary of the events in role as one of the dwarves witnessing what is happening.

Word- and Sentence-level Work

- How many synonyms can children think of for *infuriate/infuriated*? Arrange them into degrees of intensity – which will also reflect subtle differences of meaning.

- Identify, discuss and find alternatives for onomatopoeic words in the text, e.g. *whizzing, plunk, whack*.

- Investigate other ways of punctuating the text which do not use semi-colons.

- Mark the clause boundaries in the sentence *As quick as lightning they came running and swinging towards the hobbit, flinging out their long threads in all directions, till the air seemed full of waving snares.* Could the clauses be reordered/changed?

- Revise the plural of words ending in *f* like *dwarf*.

From *Peter Pan*
by J. M. Barrie

Again and again they closed upon him, and again and again he hewed a clear space. He had lifted up one boy with his hook, and was just using him as a buckler, when another, who had just passed his sword through Mullins, sprang into the fray.

"Put up your swords, boys," cried the newcomer. "This man is mine."

Thus suddenly Hook found himself face to face with Peter. The others drew back and formed a ring round them.

For long the two enemies looked at one another; Hook shuddering slightly, and Peter with the strange smile upon his face.

"So, Pan," said Hook at last, "this is all your doing."

"Aye, James Hook," came the stern answer, "it is all my doing."

"Proud and insolent youth," said Hook, "prepare to meet thy doom."

"Dark and sinister man," Peter answered, "have at thee."

Without more words they fell to, and for a space there was no advantage to either blade. Peter was a superb swordsman and parried with dazzling rapidity; ever and anon he followed up a feint with a lunge that got past his foe's defence, but his shorter reach stood him in ill stead, and he could not drive the steel home.

Shared Reading

- Does either opponent feel any anxiety about the fight? What evidence is there in the text?

- Are Peter Pan and James Hook evenly matched? What advantages and disadvantages does each one have?

- How will the fight end? Do children know?

- How would children describe the author's style?

- The word *again* is used four times in the first sentence. What is the author's purpose in doing this?

Shared Writing Activity Page

Writing a modern version.

Rewrite the extract using more up-to-date and modern English.

Other Shared Writing Ideas

Write a paragraph or two which details negative and positive reader responses to the extract (or the whole book). Ensure use of links such as *however, on the other hand, in spite of this.*

Word- and Sentence-level Work

- Identify and discuss the words and phrases which are no longer in general use or which have a different modern usage.

- Go through the text and investigate where similes and/or metaphors could be added to make the writing even more vivid.

- Identify and define technical vocabulary to do with sword-fighting – using the context and a dictionary where necessary.

- Underline the words and phrases which are used to indicate the passing of time in the extract.

- Invent a way of remembering how to spell *sword.*

Shared Text Extract 4 (Pack 10)

**From *William and the School Report*
by Richmal Crompton**

And now the last day of the term had come, and the prospect of holiday coaching loomed ominously ahead. His father had not forgotten. Only last night he had reminded William that it depended on his report whether or not he was to have lessons in the holidays ... In his pocket William carried the worst report he had ever had.

Disregarding (in common with the whole school) the headmaster's injunction to give the report to his parents without looking at it first, he had read it apprehensively in the cloak-room and it had justified his blackest fears.

He had had wild notions of altering it. The word "poor" could, he thought, easily be changed to "good", but few of the remarks stopped at "poor", and such additions as "Seems to take no interest at all in this subject" and "Work consistently ill-prepared" would read rather oddly after the comment "good".

William walked slowly and draggingly. His father would demand the report, and at once make arrangements for the holiday coaching. The four weeks of the holidays stretched – an arid desert – before him.

Shared Reading

- Was William the only pupil to have read his report? How do we know?

- What do children think – should William have read his school report? Was it wrong? Why/why not?

- Which sentence in the text indicates William's reluctance to go home and face his father?

- What might William do about the report and the prospect of extra lessons during the holiday? What would children do if they were in this situation?

Shared Writing Activity Page

Writing dialogue.

Write a script of the conversation which might have taken place between William and his father, Mr Brown, when he got home from school.

Other Shared Writing Ideas

Write William's school report – make sure that any quotations used in the extract are included. Consider which subjects he would have studied at school, e.g. bearing in mind that the story takes place in pre-computer days, so there would be no IT.

Word- and Sentence-level Work

- Identify and explain unfamiliar vocabulary such as: *coaching, ominously, injunction, apprehensively.*

- Building on from the above point, experiment with making new words from known syllabic parts.

- *The four weeks of the holidays stretched – an arid desert – before him.* Find alternative metaphors/similes to take the place of *an arid desert.*

- What simile/metaphor could be added to *William walked slowly and draggingly* to create a more powerful effect?

- Investigate the use of simple and complex sentences and when and why the former are used.

- Discuss the use of parenthetic commas, brackets and dashes in the extract.

Guided and Independent Work

Text-level Work

- The title *Facing the Enemy!* was chosen to describe the linking theme of main characters having to confront someone or something. Ask children to identify the enemy/enemies in each extract, e.g. *Oliver Twist:* Noah and his bullying; *The Hobbit:* the spiders; *A Little Princess:* Sara's poverty and Miss Minchin; *Peter Pan:* Captain Hook; *Black Beauty:* hardship of war and enemy action; *Little Women:* Hugo; *Treasure Island:* Long John Silver; *The William Stories:* the headmaster, William as his own worst enemy, his father.

- Identify the narrator in each extract. Consider if events would look the same from a different point of view.

- In which extracts are the characters experiencing real fear as opposed to apprehension or irritation?

- Discuss any film/TV versions of the books from which these extracts are taken.

- What picture of war is painted by Captain in *Black Beauty*? Would a human have had a similar view?

- How would children describe Sara's character in *A Little Princess*?

Guided Writing Ideas

Write a summary of one of the extracts in, say, 100 words. Revise this to bring the number of words down to 75 or 50.

Sentence-level Work

- Using 'An old war horse', ask the group to find examples of:
  - a simple sentence
  - a complex sentence
  - connectives, e.g. *however* on page 37
  - sentences with active and passive voices.

- Investigate transformation of the sentences children have identified, e.g. active into passive, complex into simple.

Word-level Work

- Ask children to list examples of archaic or old-fashioned vocabulary, e.g. as used in the *Peter Pan* extract.

- Invent new words from known syllabic parts which Bilbo could use to insult the spiders instead of *Attercop* in *The Hobbit* extract.

- Revise work on unstressed vowels in polysyllabic words such as *personal, immediate, violent* (page 6).

Independent Work

- Select a section of a preferred extract and rewrite it in the form of a play, using stage directions and making the setting explicit.

- Choose an extract from a novel you have read recently which fits the theme of facing an enemy. Explain why you have chosen it in not more than 30 words.

- Select one of the main characters from the extracts. Write a character description without using the character's name.

Plenary

- Select an independent activity from any of the Shared Text sections to evaluate the children's understanding and effectiveness of the task completion.

- Read some of the character descriptions. See if other children can guess the character's identity.

Copymasters

C16 Points of view

C17 Changing a passage into Standard English

Myths, Legends and Monsters

Author: *Mick Gowar*

Illustrator: *Andrew Bylo*

Genre: *four prose and one free-verse retellings of Greek and British myths and legends*

Whole Class Work

Shared Text Extract (Pack 12)

As the king sickened, so did his people and their land. It was as if hope itself had been banished. The crops rotted, unharvested, in the fields; the pigs and cattle, sickened by neglect, died in the fields. It was indeed as if the land had been cursed.

It didn't take long before some of the people began to whisper that perhaps it was time to throw off the priests and return to the ancient ways. The king should make the age-old sacrifice, they said: lay down his life that the land might become fertile again!

Childe Wynd heard the rumours and whispers. "Someone has to act," he thought. "My father can do nothing; it is up to me now as the heir to the throne."

Childe Wynd went searching for his father. He found the king in the highest tower room of the castle. There was no furniture in the room, just filthy straw on the floor. The king was sitting in the middle of the room, motionless, staring into mid-air.

"Father," said Childe Wynd. "I beg permission to go on crusade to the Holy Land. The fields are barren and the people are in despair. Maybe it is true we are accursed or bewitched. But maybe, if I go on crusade, this curse will be lifted."

"Do as you please, my boy," the king replied, with a weary sigh. "Nothing will lift the curse on me, for nothing will bring your mother back. Go if you must ... but leave me in peace."

Shared Reading

- Familiarise children with the beginning of the story.

- From what stage of the story is the text taken? (Build-up, presenting a dilemma.)

- What mood is conveyed? (Despair, gloom.) What are the main events described in the text?

- How does the author use language to create a mood, e.g. description of events, adjectives?

Shared Writing Activity Page

Comprehension and character description.

- Sentence completion.

- Write a description of the king which could be inserted into the extract after *... staring into mid-air.*

Other Shared Writing Ideas

Write a paragraph to summarise the content of the extract. Start by labelling chunks of the text with the main points or ideas.

Word- and Sentence-level Work

- Identify sentences with passive verbs.

- Discuss how the passive voice focuses attention on the object, rather than the agent; consider why and when a writer might want to do this.

- Look at punctuation in complex sentences, e.g. end of paragraphs 3 and 4.

- Experiment with rewriting/re-ordering *He found the king in the highest tower room of the castle. There was no furniture in the room, just filthy straw on the floor. The king was sitting in the middle of the room, motionless, staring into mid-air* in order to create the strongest effect.

- Investigate whether the passage can then be made stronger by the use of similes or metaphors.

Guided and Independent Work

Text-level Work

- Compare the heroes and monsters – what characteristics do each group have in common?

- The monsters are different from each other. What are the differences?

- One could say that some of the humans behave worse than some of the monsters. Which of the humans act monstrously? Who in the end are the monsters of the title?

- Look at how the author handles the passing of time, identifying key phrases, e.g. in 'The Laidly Worm'.

- In 'The Minotaur,' Theseus appears as a great hero – and he was indeed one of the great heroes of Ancient Greece. But how else does he appear in this story – besides being brave?

- Discuss the variations in style and form, e.g. addressing the reader directly (page 51), narrative poem ('Beowulf'), juxtaposition of formal narrative and colloquial dialogue 'The Sphinx', touches of humour 'The Minotaur'.

Guided Writing Ideas

Prepare pages 7–10 ('The Sphinx') as a playscript, with stage directions. Note that some events are implicit in the original text but will need to be made explicit.

Sentence-level Work

- Identify and discuss examples of active and passive voice, e.g. page 25, paragraph 1. Transform one to another.

- Revise work on complex sentences, e.g. penultimate sentence page 10 and *In between Greece ...* on page 51 which uses both dashes and brackets.

- Revise Year 5 grammar by re-expressing sentences from 'Beowulf' in a modern, narrative form.

- Summarise the opening, e.g. of 'The Laidly Worm', in no more than five sentences.

- Look at the language forms used to sequence the events on pages 22–23.

- Identify the function of the conditionals *could* and *would* on page 55.

Word-level Work

- Introduce the study of proverbs by discussing the character of Theseus in terms of the proverb 'Handsome is as handsome does'.

- Write short stories to illustrate other proverbs.

- List words and phrases which would be useful in arguing whether or not Theseus is presented as a true hero, e.g. *similarly, on the other hand, therefore, it appears that.*

- Collect descriptive or powerful verbs, e.g. *banished* (page 20), *screaming, retching, oozed* (page 22), to practise and extend vocabulary.

- Consolidate spellings of unstressed vowels in polysyllabic words, e.g. *treasure, laughter, humankind, vengeance, fierceness* in 'Beowulf'.

Independent Work

- Transform passive sentences from the text to the active voice; change a number of active sentences to the passive voice.

- Draft a new passage for the extract where the opposite mood (optimistic) is conveyed, with different events.

- You are Ariadne, abandoned on Naxos. Write a farewell letter to your family, explaining what has happened. Will you ask them to avenge your death?

Plenary

- Read some of the children's new passages and discuss their use of the passive voice.

- Identify reasons for using the passive voice; collect examples from other texts.

Copymasters

C19 Character study

C20 Writing a description using simile and metaphor

White Bird Flying

Author: *Nicholas Orme*

Illustrator: *Hemesh Alles*

Genre: *historical short stories, set in the same fictitious village, from King Alfred's time up to the present*

Whole Class Work

Shared Text Extract (Pack 12)

The Poacher and the Pie

"Hello, Fursdon," called the earl. "Good day for a ride, what? How's the poaching?"

Mr Fursdon bounded forward eagerly, "My Lord!" he cried. "I've dealt with one today. Caught on your very own property. I've just been writing a note to tell you."

"What! Bagged one of the bounders who've been plaguing me?" said the earl. "Who caught him? None of my men reported anything."

"Constable Clumber brought him in this morning," said Mr Fursdon. "Fellow from this village. Handwich."

The earl whistled. "By Gad. He's an old offender, isn't he? Anything on him?"

"Two brace of pheasants," said the magistrate. "They're in my stable."

The earl slid down from the saddle and gave his reins to the groom. "Let's see," he said. "I always like to know what these fellows are after."

They walked round the house to the stables. Mr Fursdon took down the bag and held it open triumphantly. The early peered in. "Handsome birds, Fursdon," he said. He gave a snort. "Only trouble is, they aren't mine."

"What!" said the magistrate.

"Absolutely not. This is a fancy variety. Golden Wonders. We don't rear 'em. Wherever your poacher found 'em it wasn't my woods."

"Are you sure?" asked Mr Fursdon incredulously.

"Quite. Nobody round here has 'em. The Duke does, but that's forty miles away. If your poacher bagged 'em there, he's working on a pretty big scale." The earl was losing interest. "Got to go," he said. "Countess wants me. Dinner party."

Shared Reading

- Read 'The Poacher and the Pie' up to the top of page 142. Secure the plot so far and identify the main characters.

- Establish children's understanding of poaching in this context.

- Explore the relationships between the characters in the piece, identifying passages of text to support opinions.

- Identify the setting.

- Discuss what might be an appropriate voice in which to read each character's speeches. Does any of the reading aloud demand exaggeration?

Shared Writing Activity Page

Parody.

- Discuss the way the earl speaks and how this reflects his character.

- Write the conversation that might have taken place between the earl and the countess in which he tells her about his meeting with the magistrate.

Other Shared Writing Ideas

I've just been writing a note to tell you ... Write the magistrate's note to the earl. Will it, in fact, be as informal as the word *note* suggests?

Word- and Sentence-level Work

- Consider the features of the earl's speech, e.g. staccato sentences. How does this reflect the earl's character? Is this a parody?

- Discuss the earl's final speech. How could this be extended into a complex sentence?

- Look at the expressions used by the earl, e.g. *bagged one of the bounders,* and ascertain their meaning from the text.

- Write two definitions of the verb *poach*.

Guided and Independent Work

Text-level Work

- Read the first and the last story. The place is the same, but identify elements which tell the reader that years have passed, e.g. language, names, events.

- The White Bird appears in the first and last stories. What might the white bird be?

- 'The Way to Jerusalem' ends with a twist (pages 75–79). Consider the Vicar's story. Could he be telling the truth?

- Write a time line for the village of Brierleigh, indicating the main events in its history.

- Explore the biblical text referred to on pages 121–122. Discuss what it means and whether it might help Verity.

- Do the stories have any thread which runs through them all?

Guided Writing Ideas

Identify the common elements that occur throughout the stories. Use these to write a further episode about the village, set in the future, and written in the style of futuristic tales from previous reading.

Sentence-level Work

- Investigate prepositions and connectives on page 69, such as *however, on, behind*.

- Look at *they were given ...* (page 97) as an example of a passive verb. Consider how the agent of the sentence is concealed.

- Investigate the complex sentences in the first paragraph on page 105. Rewrite them in simple sentences using single clauses.

- Note the use of the conditional form at the bottom of page 101, and explore transforming as if Luke had posed the question.

- Identify examples of formal language used in the mortgage document on page 123. Consider the form and style. Compare with other examples of official documentation.

Word-level Work

- Identify new words such as *bloke* (page 159), *burgers* (page 165).

- Revise diminutive forms from Year 4, looking at *kid* (page 157) and *handkerchief* (page 162).

- The family visit a store called 'Sainsworth' (page 159). Create names for other shops using syllabic parts, e.g. 'Asco', 'Dixet'. What would these shops sell?

- Explore the spelling of words using the prefix *ex*, e.g. *expensive, examining* on page 157.

- Collect and explore the spelling patterns of words ending in *ion*, e.g. *invitation* (page 105), *possession* (page 156) and note any changes when there is a further addition, e.g. *congratulations* (page 42), *educational* (page 156).

Independent Work

- Write up Handwich's arrest from different points of view, e.g. as a newspaper headline, Clumber's arrest report, Sam's own story, the earl to his wife.

- Explore extending the telegram on page 143, classifying the types of additions made, e.g. adverbs, causal connectives such as *because*.

Plenary

- Read the children's extended telegrams. Discuss why these would not be appropriate and point out how the meaning has become less clear.

- Compare the different points of view, exploring elements of bias and persuasive argument.

Copymasters

C23 Questions about the book

C24 Changing active into passive and vice versa

On the Day the World Began

Author: *Geraldine McCaughrean*
Illustrator: *Norman Bancroft Hunt*
Genre: *fourteen creation myths within a linking framework*

Whole Class Work

Shared Text Extract 1 (Pack 12)

Adrift

One day in time, and at one turn of the tide, there arose such weather as whirled the world around and washed out of shape both time and tide. The Past presented itself where it was least expected. The calendar months were derailed, all twelve, shunting May into March and August into Autumn.

The globe, like a rubbed balloon, clung to the sky by electrical magic. Tides tugged icebergs and islands about the great circles of the Earth. And men and women from all times and places dreamed they were blown like the leaves from the trees and squandered across the ocean.

In a sleep-rumpled sea beneath a blanketing fog, a small raft tossed and turned – a square of planks such as Noah might have used for a gangplank. A hand reached over its edge and fumbled for a hold. Then another on the other side.

Out from beneath twenty different waves, a whole shoal of swimmers closed on the raft and began to pull themselves aboard, gasping and choking. Each was startled to see the others, but it was no time to pick or choose one's companions.

Shared Reading

- Explain that this is the introduction to a book in which a group of people tell the story of the creation according to their own time, culture and beliefs.

- What is being described? Is it a natural phenomenon? How do we know?

- How effective is this as an opening to a book?

- How would children describe the author's style of writing? Point out to children that this is writing of exceptional quality from an award-winning author.

Shared Writing Activity Page

Imagery.

- Go through the text and underline and discuss all the examples of similes and metaphors.

- Which image do most people think is the most effective?

- Write a description of a fierce storm. First decide on the setting (at sea? in the country?) and whether it will be at night or in daylight.

Other Shared Writing Ideas

List similes and metaphors which could be used to describe another cataclysmic event such as an earthquake.

Word- and Sentence-level Work

- Identify uses of the passive voice, e.g. *dreamed they were blown like the leaves.*

- Identify the main and subordinate clauses, e.g. in *The calendar months were derailed, all twelve, shunting May into March and August into Autumn.*

- Discuss the use of simile and metaphor in creating powerful images in the text.

- Identify words with prefixes and suffixes. Generate other examples using the same prefix/suffix.

"In perfecting his art, Creator made a great many jungles, deserts and plains. Each mountain was bigger and more beautiful than the last, each landscape more picturesque. But in the joy of making, Creator piled just too many things aboard the island Earth. It started to sink under the weight. The mountains were simply too full of gold and precious jewels, the jungles were just too busy with trampling elephants. For a time it seemed as if the whole of Creation might capsize, and everything slip back into the sea.

"Then Creator asked Snake to help him. 'Coil yourself into a circle and lie beneath the world to steady it,' he said.

"So Great Snake slipped silently under the listing world, coiling himself round and round, holding it firm and fast. The Earth no longer rolled about, and the work of Creator was saved. Creator charged a tribe of red monkeys (who lived in the sea already) to keep the Snake fed with his favourite food. So from the mines of the oceans they fetched iron bars, night and day, to keep up the serpent's strength.

"Of course, the Snake never stops moving, so that as he swims in a circle, the Earth is turned round and round. That's why the stars appear to move in the sky. But such circlings are smooth. Only rarely does Snake sneeze or cough or writhe in a restless dream. Then the coils are set rippling in his monstrous scaly back, and the Earth above shakes and the ground splits open and mountains crumble and fall."

Shared Reading

- Why did the Creator need the Snake?

- What is the Snake's favourite food? Why were the red monkeys chosen to feed him?

- What is the significance of the opening phase *In perfecting his art*? Does it explain why the Earth became overloaded?

- What natural phenomena is the myth attempting to explain (the rotation of the Earth, earthquakes)?

Shared Writing Activity Page

Writing in the style of the author.

Extend the myth in the style of the author to explain hurricanes.

Other Shared Writing Ideas

Write a brief synopsis of the text.

Word- and Sentence-level Work

- Which words are difficult to understand? Can children guess meanings from the parts of the words? Check meanings in a dictionary.

- Use *picturesque* to initiate the study of words ending in *que: unique, antique, oblique, pique, clique, opaque.*

- Investigate the spellings of words formed by adding prefixes and suffixes to *create,* e.g. *creator, creation, creative, creatively, procreate.*

- Discuss the meaning of *listing* in this context. What other meaning can the word have? Can children find another word which is not used in its more common sense? (*fast*) How many meanings for this word do they know?

Guided and Independent Work

Text-level Work

- The Christian clergyman is surprised at how similar some of the stories are. What similarities can children find in these stories from all over the world?

- As the characters wait on the raft for the end, the scientist is the only one who is unhappy. Why is this?

- Compare two myths, their content – i.e. where they are set, who is involved, how the myth develops – and their style of narration, i.e. is it written in a simple or an ornate style?

- Discuss creation stories from different cultures that children already know. Ask them to narrate them to the class.

- Model and write the characteristics of such stories after discussion. Do they have any characteristics in common?

Guided Writing Ideas

Plan and begin the transformation of one of the children's stories into a playscript. Take the opportunity to revise the rules for writing of scripts.

Sentence-level Work

- Examine sentence structure: repetition for effect, e.g. page 11, *come back, for a long time.*

- Consider the use of simple, short sentences for dramatic effect on page 21.

- Compare use of commas and semi-colons (page 24) in different kinds of lists.

- Develop this discussion of punctuation into the use of colons (page 33) for introducing, rather than continuing an idea.

- Identify and list a range of connectives, e.g. page 32, and discuss their effect in making complex sentences.

Word-level Work

- List and examine origins of new 'scientific' words, e.g. pages 89–90.

- List and examine astronomical words, e.g. *galaxy, universe.*

- List and examine science words, e.g. *condensation, atmosphere, protein, radiation, hydrogen.*

- Consider prefixes and word roots as a help to meaning, e.g. page 89: *universe – uni* means *one, atmosphere* from Latin, *solar* from the sun, etc.

- Collect new words from the stories – those from different cultures and religions. Make word lists from other areas of the curriculum.

- Consider words developed from people's names, e.g. *shrapnel.* Do some work with etymological dictionaries.

Independent Work

- Children could list ways of saying something simple, e.g. *hello*, for a variety of audiences.

- When is slang appropriate?

- Create more sentences where the colon is used to introduce a new idea or a list.

- List words which have changed over time and have gone out of use, e.g. *yonder, thither.*

- Complete the transformation of one of the stories into a playscript.

Plenary

- Assess and monitor children's awareness of suitable styles for appropriate audiences by discussing their lists of ways of saying things.

- Check understanding of the use of the colon when children are giving their examples.

- List any old-fashioned phrases and make a language curiosity word wall.

Copymasters

C27 Presenting one story in summary text and pictures

C28 Rewriting narrative as explanatory text

Weaving Words: poems in different forms

Author: *selected by David Orme*

Illustrators: *Rosalind Hudson, Brian Lee and Maggie Ling*

Genre: *poems in different forms, arranged in thematic pairs*

Whole Class Work

Shared Text Extract 1 (Pack 10)

***Witches' Chant** from Macbeth*
by William Shakespeare

Round about the cauldron go:
In the poisoned entrails throw.

Toad, that under cold stone
Days and nights has thirty-one

Sweated venom sleeping got,
Boil thou first in the charmed pot.

Double, double toil and trouble:
Fire burn and cauldron bubble.

Fillet of a fenny snake,
In the cauldron boil and bake;

Eye of newt and toe of frog,
Wool of bat and tongue of dog,

Adder's fork and blindworm's sting,
Lizard's leg and owlet's wing.

For a charm of powerful trouble,
Like a hell-broth boil and bubble.

Double, double toil and trouble
Fire burn and cauldron bubble.

Scale of dragon, tooth of wolf,
Witch's mummy, maw and gulf

Of the ravenous salt-sea shark,
Root of hemlock digged in the dark,

Make the gruel thick and slab:
Add thereto a tiger's chaudron,

For the ingredients of our cauldron.

Double, double toil and trouble:
Fire burn and cauldron bubble.

Shared Reading

- Do children find the chant menacing? Why/why not?

- Which line indicates that it is the witches who are speaking? (*our cauldron*).

- Identify and discuss the rhyming scheme – representing it with A A, etc.

- Where is the rhyme weak? Why is this so?

Shared Writing Activity Page

Writing in the style of the poet.

- List all the pleasant things which could form ingredients to cancel out the Witches' Chant, e.g. the smile of a baby; the song of a bird.

- Use the list to write a poem starting:
  Make those witches' power abate,
  Gather to you what they hate.
  Witches loathe what mortals love:

Other Shared Writing Ideas

Write a description of the three witches who are making the spell.

Word- and Sentence-level Work

- Identify and discuss the meanings of all the unfamiliar words. Write a glossary, e.g.
  – *mummy*: preparation made originally from mummies and used as a medicine as well as for magical purposes
  – *maw and gulf*: stomach and gullet
  – *chaudron*: entrails
  – *slab*: slimy

- Translate the third verse into modern English. Which verb form will have to change? What could be used instead of *thereto*?

Meg Merrilies *by John Keats*

Old Meg she was a gipsy;
  And lived upon the moors:
Her bed it was the brown heath turf,
  And her house was out of doors.
Her apples were swart blackberries,
  Her currants pods o' broom;
Her wine was dew of the wild white rose,
  Her book a churchyard tomb.

Her brothers were the craggy hills,
  Her sisters larchen trees;
Alone with her great family
  She lived as she did please.
No breakfast had she many a morn,
  No dinner many a noon,
And 'stead of supper, she would stare
  Full hard against the moon.

But every morn, of woodbine fresh
  She made her garlanding,
And, every night, the dark yew glen
  She wove, and she would sing.
And with her fingers, old and brown,
  She plaited mats of rushes,
And gave them to the cottagers
  She met among the bushes.

Old Meg was brave as Margaret Queen,
  and tall as Amazon;
An old red blanket cloak she wore,
  A chip-hat had she on;
God rest her aged bones somewhere –
  She died full long agone!

Shared Reading

- Discuss Meg's lifestyle – what did she eat, drink, read? What did she have as a substitute for relatives?

- What does *tall as Amazon* mean? (Children may think it refers to the river.)

- How could Meg's character be described – Strong? Carefree? Lonely? Solitary? Friendly? Generous?

- Does the poet admire Meg? How do we know?

- Identify and discuss the rhyming scheme – representing it with A B C B, etc.

- Where is the rhyme weak? Why is this so?

Shared Writing Activity Page

Character study.

If Meg Merrilies was living in the present, how would her life be different? Write a poetic description of her and her life as if she was a homeless person in a city. Would the mood of your description differ from that of the poem?

Other Shared Writing Ideas

Write a physical description of Meg and how she might have looked.

Word- and Sentence-level Work

- Identify and discuss the meanings of all the unfamiliar words. Write a glossary, e.g.
  – *swart:* black, dark-coloured
  – *chip-hat:* hat or bonnet made of straw or thin strips of wood/wood fibre.

- Identify which lines have missing verbs, e.g. *Her book a churchyard tomb.* Why is this? What effect does putting in the verb have?

- Discuss the meanings and experiment with different ways of saying: *many a morn; she would stare / Full hard against the moon; tall as Amazon; full long agone*

- What does *o'* stand for?

Guided and Independent Work

Text-level Work

- Point out that anthologists can structure anthologies in different ways. Discuss how successful the idea of pairing poems is in this anthology.

- Choose any pair of poems and determine children's preferences. Ask them to justify their choice quoting from the poem to support their view.

- Discuss and compare the forms and structures of the various poems.

- Find and discuss examples of personification eg 'The Beach' (page 5).

- How does the poet give a sense of the speed of movement of a cat in 'Nick's Cat' (page 21)? Do the single-syllable, short vowel phonemes help? Compare with 'Cat' (page 22).

- Make sure children realise there are hidden words in 'Where?' on page 22!

Guided Writing Ideas

- Plan and write an extension to the poem 'The Beach' using personification to describe the sea turning its attention and working with the wind to wreck a ship.

Sentence-level Work

- Investigate the use of punctuation in the poems. How might 'Night Mer' have been additionally punctuated had the poet decided to do so?

- Experiment with expanding the short lines in 'Nick's Cat' into fuller, more complex sentences. How does this alter the impact of the poem?

- Experiment with isolating the main clause in a complex sentence, checking that it will stand on its own.

Word-level Work

- In 'Wave' (page 4), has the poet made up any words? Use a dictionary to check.

- Discuss how the poet has created hyphenated words to strengthen the description in 'Winter' (page 14) and 'A Windy Day' (page 9). Create hyphenated words to describe one of the seasons.

- 'Translate' 'Night Mer' on page 32. Discuss how the poet has created these new words and generate some further examples.

Independent Work

- Write a poem which hides words within the lines, like 'Where?' on page 22.

- Create hyphenated words to describe a wild animal.

Plenary

Evaluate the success of the poems and the lists of hyphenated words.

Copymasters

C36 Comparing two poems

C37 Rewriting a poem as a story introduction

Tales from the Underland

Author: *Dennis Hamley*
Illustrator: *Michaela Blunden*
Genre: *traditional stories from the British Isles, all involving Faeryland or the Underland*

Whole Class Work

Shared Text Extract (Pack 12)

King O'Hara's Youngest Daughter

Years ago, a king lived in Desmond in Ireland and his name was King Coluath O'Hara. This king had, besides his queen and his kingdom, four great responsibilities. One of them, he was sure, would some day lead him into deep trouble. The first responsibility was a magic cloak which came from who knows where and had been handed down the generations. It gave great power to anyone who put it on so it had to be used very carefully. The other three responsibilities were his daughters.

One day, King Coluath O'Hara and his queen had to go away to sort out some royal business.

The king's last words to his daughters were: "Don't interfere with my magic cloak." So, as soon as they were out of sight, the eldest daughter said, "Where is it?"

She was tired of living in her parents' castle and wanted freedom. The only way she could think of to get it was to find a husband and live in his castle.

She found the magic cloak in the king's wardrobe, put it on and said: "I wish for the most handsome man in Ireland to be my husband."

The result was amazing. No sooner had she put the cloak back than a golden coach with two black horses and two white horses pulled up outside the castle.

Shared Reading

- Before working on the shared text, read the author's introduction and ask the children to predict style, themes and characters.

- Read the extract. How does the opening paragraph help the reader to predict the development?

- What power does the cloak seem to possess?

- Is the story likely to concentrate on this daughter? Why/Why not? (The title).

- What other alternatives to freedom might the daughter have considered? Is her solution a reasonable one?

- Identify elements of traditional stories, e.g. three daughters, a magical object. Discuss how these elements might be developed in the story.

Shared Writing Activity Page

Descriptive writing.

- What the cloak might look like.

- The magic powers it might have.

Other Shared Writing Ideas

Plan and start to write diary entries for the eldest daughter.

Word- and Sentence-level Work

- Look at the king's surname *O'Hara*. Brainstorm what the origin might be (Irish origin, meaning *son of*) and compare with other known examples, e.g. *MacDonald* and *Magnusson*.

- Investigate the use of clauses in the second and third sentences. Identify the main clauses.

- Revise the use of possessive apostrophes for plural nouns, e.g. *her parents' castle*.

- Identify uses of the colon – what alternative punctuation mark might have been used instead?

Guided and Independent Work

Text-level Work

- Use the author's introduction to predict the elements of the stories, e.g. characters, themes, structure, based on previous reading.

- 'Elidor knew time was different in the two worlds' (page 129). Find evidence in the text to support this.

- Read the last page. Write what might happen if the entrance was rediscovered.

- Look at the chapter titles in 'Pwyll, Prince of Dyfed' (pages 61–85). How do these help the reader identify the links between the chapters?

- Consider the opening paragraphs of each of the stories, looking at how they are structured to introduce and involve the reader from the outset.

Guided Writing Ideas

Rewrite the events of May Eve (pages 78–80) as a playscript.

Sentence-level Work

- Identify connecting words and phrases on page 50, such as *under, next to, beside, in front of.*

- Discuss the functions of dashes, colons and parenthetic commas on page 85.

- Rewrite Pwyll and Rhiannon's conversation on page 71 as reported speech. Note the grammar conventions needed.

- Collect examples of conditionals, e.g. 'How could this girl ...?' (page 87), which pose a question or dilemma for the reader and set the scene for the story.

- In 'Pwyll, Prince of Dyfed', identify connecting words and phrases that sequence the events at the start of paragraphs, e.g. *at last* (page 66) *meanwhile* (page 68).

Word-level Work

- Use *company* and *deserve* on page 56 to revise work on unstressed vowels from Year 5.

- At the end of page 33, discuss what is meant by 'may we all ... fare as well ...' Explore how this usage has changed over time, and the present-day equivalents. Discuss the origin of the word 'fare' (from the Norse word meaning to 'travel').

- Use *consciousness* on page 89 to identify the prefix *con*. Brainstorm and list other examples, e.g. *concert, concentrate*. Note the use of the soft *c* in the second syllable.

- Look at the syllabic parts of place names, such as 'Winchester' (page 17) and 'Orkney' (page 115). Generate and explore placenames with the same roots, e.g. 'Manchester', 'Hackney'.

Independent Work

- Complete the diary entries for the eldest daughter.

- List the main clauses in given sentences, e.g. the opening paragraph of the extract.

- Collect and classify names of children in the class or from known reading. Look for common syllables, and explore spelling conventions.

- If you had to edit this book to half its length, which stories would you keep and which ones would you cut? Why?

Plenary

- Display the collection of names, and add to this as more examples are collected.

- Explore the rule for main clauses, i.e. that a main clause stands on its own as a simple sentence.

- Compare children's responses to the editing out stories task. Could they adequately justify their choices?

Copymasters

C31 Questions about the book

C32 Word meanings

The Quest of Isis

Author: *Geraldine McCaughrean*
Illustrator: *David Sim*
Genre: *myth from Ancient Egypt*

Whole Class Work

Shared Text Extract (Pack 12)

Son-rise

"I must find him before he stifles! I must find him! I must!" cried Isis aloud, into the shock-white face of the Moon. Her tears fell and startled little tufts of dust up off the dry street. Dark drops of dampness patterned the ground around her feet, then joined together into puddles. And still Isis wept. Into the cracked desert trickled Isis' tears, startling beetles and scorpions out of hiding. And still Isis wept. Legless fish stirred and wriggled in the mud. The mud turned to pools. Gullies bubbled full of water. And still Isis wept. "Oh my brother!

My husband! Where are you? Oh people, creatures! Help me find him!"

The Nile, a sluggish, yellow streak of a stream, was swelled by her tears. It rose and set afloat the crocodiles basking along its banks. It washed away dead trees and fallen branches. It rose and continued to rise, for nothing could comfort Isis or stop her weeping. As the river burst its banks, cool snakes woke to find their hot scales hissing and swam for high ground. The wild cattle and tame cows plodded, hock-deep, into the hills. Soon every dune and mound was crowned with a cluster of men and beasts cut off by the rising water. But Isis saw nothing of this: her eyes were too full of tears.

Shared Reading

- Ensure the children have heard or read the story up to page 18. Secure the main characters, theme and setting.

- Discuss the chapter heading. What indication does this give of what could happen next?

- Consider how this extract is a mythical representation of a natural phenomenon. Will Isis' tears bring about a positive outcome?

- Underline those parts of the text which are particularly effective in creating the mood and strength of emotion.

- What could happen next? Bear in mind mythical and magical events in such stories, and the way these were designed to explain events in the natural world.

Shared Writing Activity Page

Language features.

- How many examples of the following language features can you find? How do they add to the effectiveness of the writing? – alliteration, repetition, onomatopoeia, assonance, compound word, metaphor and personification.

- Describe *crocodiles* using some of the above features

Other Shared Writing Ideas

Write two descriptions of Isis conveying her grief, as she would appear to an onlooker – first to someone who disliked her and then to someone who cared about her.

Word- and Sentence-level Work

- Explore the use of the homophone *son* in the chapter heading as a pun on the phrase *sun-rise*. Ask the children if they can give any other examples, particularly from advertising.

- Look at the repetition of the sentence *And still Isis wept*. Discuss why the author has used this repetitive style and why, in this instance, it is acceptable to start a sentence with a connective.

- Explore the sequence of events, identifying the words and phrases that indicate the build up, e.g. *as, soon*.

Guided and Independent Work

Text-level Work

- This story is called a quest. What is a quest? What other books featuring quests do children know?

- Use a storyboard or comic strip format to isolate the main events of the quest, using as few points as possible.

- Read Chapter 2. Examine Set's motives. What made him behave as he did?

- Compare this story with other versions of the same myth. What are the common features? Isolate similarities and differences.

- How well do the illustrations portray the setting and culture? How historically accurate are they? How do you know?

Guided Writing Ideas

Use the features of myths to plan new stories which explain natural phenomena, such as the seasons, tidal patterns.

Sentence-level Work

- Identify the use of ellipses to mark interruptions and pauses on page 8. Compare with the use of dashes on the next page.

- Compare the grammatical conventions, e.g. tenses, used in the introduction (page 5) with the story text.

- Look at the use of possessive apostrophes for words ending in s on page 35.

- Read the conversations on pages 32 and 33 to pinpoint evidence of formal language, such as imperative verbs and formal address.

- Experiment with changing the order of clauses and sentences in the paragraph beginning *In a flurry of flying robes ...* on page 33.

Word-level Work

- Explore the words *sarcophagus* and *sarcophagi* on page 45, looking at syllabic parts and plural endings. Also see page 16, *hippopotami*.

- Look for examples of words using the *ex* prefix, such as *excitement* (page 16), *exhausted* (page 23).

- Use *intelligence* (page 13) and *husband* (page 33) as examples of unstressed vowels. Discuss strategies for spelling these words.

- Note *hither and yon* (page 41) as an example of a phrase that has changed over time. Use the context to ascertain the modern-day equivalent.

- Identify the syllabic parts of *unfaithfulness* (page 11) and discuss the spelling conventions used here.

Independent Work

- Ask the children to write their own myth to explain why rivers flood.

- Using a copy of the extract, or acetate over the page, highlight the main point of each paragraph. List and order these using a range of connectives.

- Illustrate funny puns which use homophones.

- Isis tells her story to the king (page 32). Write in the role of Isis, explaining what has happened so far. Predict how the king will respond.

Plenary

- Display the homophone pictures and add to the collection from newspapers and magazines.

- Compare the children's myths with other stories about floods.

- Look at the main points. Can these be contracted any further?

Copymasters

C34 Finding the main events

C35 Editing down and writing a summary of a passage

Today, as never before, children grow up in a multi-media society. From their earliest days, they experience the impact of fast-moving, colourful and sometimes transient images which both fascinate and teach. Yet watching a television screen is largely a passive activity; it is both easy and effortless because control is mainly vested outside the child. Someone else has created or selected the images and determined the rate and nature of their presentation.

Reading a book, however, requires effort. It also places control in the hands and mind of the reader, for, at their own pace, readers construct the world of the book inside their own heads, weaving their own images and shaping their own responses.

The people we encounter on the page can prepare us for those we meet in life, and the literature, language and learning we experience through books are a unique means of exploring or extending our emotions, language use and intellect. We can explore at will, unfettered by time or place or even death, for through print a voice can last for centuries. The words and minds of millions are ours to discover because, whether it was placed on the page by quill or computer, the written word has permanency.

To read, then, is to have control, and to have control over the written word is to have power – the power not only to sample and consider other people's words, ideas and views but also, in turn, to reach out to others with our own words.

Writers will always reach out to readers with books ... for although we can communicate with computers, we cannot curl up with them.

Just as we make this richness and power of print available to children by teaching them to read and write, so should we celebrate the book as the longest standing, most powerful and flexible means of entering other worlds and other minds.

The Longman Book Project was created to develop children's language and learning skills. But it also endeavours to place books and all they stand for firmly at the heart of language teaching and learning. For books are more than just vehicles for teaching literacy skills, they can also bring about that fascination with the written word which will help all children to feel like Martin Tupper (1810–89) when he said: *A good book is the best of friends ...*

This book is part of

THE LONGMAN BOOK PROJECT

General Editor Sue Palmer
Fiction Editor Wendy Body
Non-fiction Editor Bobbie Neate

Pearson Education Limited
Edinburgh Gate
Harlow
Essex
CM20 2JE
England

© Pearson Education Limited 2000

The right of Wendy Body to be identified as the author of this Work has been asserted by her in accordance with the Copyright, Designs and Patents Act of 1988.

All rights reserved; no part of this publication may be reproduced, stored in a retrieval system, or transmitted in any form or by any means, electronic, mechanical, photocopying, recording, or otherwise without either the prior written permission of the Publishers or a licence permitting restricted copying in the United Kingdom issued by the Copyright Licensing Agency Ltd, 90 Tottenham Court Road, London, W1P 9HE, with the exception of Copymasters

ISBN 0582 428025

First published 2000

Printed in China

Designed by Ken Vail Graphic Design, Cambridge

The Publisher's policy is to use paper manufactured from sustainable forests.